Your Forgotten Child

A journey returning to love and innocence

Sweet Pickle Books
47 Orchard Street
New York, NY 10002

Mercedes Guzman

Copyright © 2019 by Mercedes Guzman
All rights reserved

This book, or parts thereof, may not be reproduced in any form without permission from the publisher except for brief excerpts used for reviews.

Published by MBG Greater Possibilities
www.mercedesguzman.com

ISBN 10: 1-937985-56-3
ISBN 13: 978-1-937985-56-1
eBook ISBN 10: 1-937985-55-5
eBook ISBN 13: 978-1-937985-55-4

Printed in the U.S.A.

Cover designed by Daniel Arzola – www.facebook.com/Arzoladaniel Design collaboration back cover Natalia Ruiz – www.dynmkstudio.co

The names of the people in this book have been changed to protect their privacy.

This is a work of nonfiction based on the author's personal experiences, case studies, and interviews with people concerning their inner child experiences. Any similarity between fictitious names used and those of living personas is entirely coincidental.

Acknowledgments

There is a Divine Presence which fills my soul, my being, my spirit, and strengthens me every day. To this presence I give thanks.

Infinite thanks to my husband, Daniel Guzman. Alongside him, our inner children have found the road to return to love and innocence. With his love, he took the role of a husband who has shown me the pain that I had been holding in my subconscious, and with his patience, our relationship continues to grow more and more. I love you.

To my children, Yanica, Lia, Zelzen, Gerson, and Enoc, who chose me in this time and space to be my teachers, my friends, and my companions. Through them, I am able to see this life with a magical perspective. The love that I feel while being in their presence is indescribable. They have been the medium through which I have been able to connect with my inner child in a celestial way. You are the force that keeps me going each day.

To my parents, Ana Mercedes and Juan Antonio, for giving me life and teaching me so many beautiful principles like responsibility, honesty, and service to others. You have made me into the woman that I am today.

To my siblings, Bety, Daysi, Mauricio, Carlos, I love you for being a part of my childhood and my life. My uncles, aunts, cousins, grandparents, and my whole family tree, now that I understand your experiences, I thank you.

To Xochitl Lopez, my soul sister, for dreaming with me ever since I was twenty-six years old. Together we have evolved, and she was the one who listened to and saw my vision in the beginning of my career, and never doubted me.

To Claudia Valenzuela, my friend, for your support and love.

To every person who has formed part of my spiritual growth, thank you.

What Your Inner Child Teaches You

Your inner child is very real and is connected to everything and everyone.

Your inner child helps you to remember who you are: a being of light, pure and perfect.

Your inner child creates from love or can create from fear, and the world will show you his or her creations.

There is no age to liberate your inner child. It can be at ten years old, twenty years old, or ninety years old.

Your inner child can heal your illnesses, let go of fears and resentments.

Your inner child can help you to forgive even the person who deserves it the least.

Your inner child can attract the right and perfect job or business for you.

Your inner child has the magic to let go of all your unnecessary weight.

Your inner child has the magic to raise your self-esteem.

Your inner child has the magic to free your anxieties and fears.

Your inner child knows how to create limitless miracles.

CONTENTS

Chapter 1: Reconnecting With
My Inner Child 1
    *How did I begin my journey of the
inner child?*..4
    Back to the childhood............................13
    My inner child and the prostitutes 15
    My inner child and exclusion 17
    My inner child and her father...................20
    My inner child and religion......................22
    My inner child and Santa Claus..............24
    My inner child and death 24
    My inner child, guilt and shame..............26
    My inner child and witches 28

Chapter 2: The Subconscious
Mind – Inner Child 30
    *Life is governed by laws and
principles* 33

Chapter 3: My Inner Child at
Seven Years Old..37
    *Patterns of behavior created
to survive*..43

Chapter 4: Loss of Memory and
Your Inner Child 45

Chapter 5: To Bless or Condemn and
Your Inner Child 48

Chapter 6: It Was Not Your Fault,
It Never Was 52

Chapter 7: Your Inner Child and Money 65

Chapter 8: Your Inner Child and
Your Relationships 77

Chapter 9: Your Inner Child and
Sexual Orientation 90

   Relationships in gay couples 96

Chapter 10: Your Inner Child and Health 97

Chapter 11: Parents Can Create
Illnesses in Their Children 101

Chapter 12: Your Inner Child and
Sickness 104

Chapter 13: Success and
Your Inner Child 110

Chapter 14: Practical Exercises to
Reconnect With Your Forgotten Child 119

   *Let your inner child tell you how
they feel 119*

   Speak with your inner child 119

Your inner child will help you with relationship problems 120
Your inner child will help you with financial issues 120
You can teach your inner child kindness 121
Your inner child needs tender and stimulating words 122
Involve your inner child in your life daily 122
Your inner child needs to develop patience 123
Journey back in time with your inner child 123

Conclusion 126

Bibliography 129

Preface

Arthur was a fifteen-year-old boy when I first met him. Not knowing what else to do, his parents brought him to speak with me. They told me that Arthur had not passed the ninth grade and now, in the new school year, he was failing some classes, which meant that if he continued in this manner, he would once again have to repeat the year.

Speaking with Arthur, I could see a very educated, super intelligent, quick to smile young boy who loved sports. He had wonderful parents who really loved and cared for him. However, the attitude that Arthur had when it came to his studies was one of "I don't care." He did not feel accepted by his classmates, and a lot of the time he would do things that would get him into trouble. This, he would do unknowingly, in order to gain favor and acceptance from the others. In our sessions, I observed how the issue was that he really did not accept himself and he had low self-esteem.

When we had a chance to connect with his inner child, we were able to see that most of these issues started when he was six years old, when his family had to move. The move also meant that he would have to attend a new school, which is where he encountered his first problem.

During lunch, a kid decided to push Arthur while he was walking, causing him to fall. The manner in which he fell caused his ear to tear, and kids started to laugh at him. Because of the physical trauma, the act of being bullied, as well as the situation going on with his family, that moment triggered a feeling of pain for him, which led him to begin looking at school as a painful place. He became a rebellious kid without any desire to study. This simply added to his parents' stress, who in that moment could not see what he was actually going through or why he was acting out.

During our conversations, I showed him how to regain his self-respect and how to apply it in his life. With a new decision to change, as well as new-found self-esteem, he was able to change his attitude. After a few years, I received a message from his mother informing me that he had graduated from school with honors.

> *"Your inner child is very real with all of its creative innocence, self-love, pride, feeling of belonging, and beauty."* —Mercedes Guzman

In the preface of Anthony de Mello's book, *Awareness,* there is a story that applies to the majority of us in relation to what was programmed in us as children. This is the reason why it is so difficult for us to accept our greatness and why we live mediocre lives without meaning. Once we understand who we are, reconnect and reprogram our inner child, we can truly become limitless once again.

> *There was a man who once found an eagle egg. Taking the egg, he placed it in a nest in his chicken coop. The eagle hatched alongside the other baby chicks and grew up with them. The eagle spent his whole life doing the exact same thing that the chickens did. He scraped the dirt in search of worms and bugs. He made the same sounds as a chicken, and when he flapped his wings, he even flew like a chicken.*

> *The years passed, and the eagle aged. One day he looked up and saw a beautiful bird flying through the sky. The bird flew with ease, sailing on the different air currents with its strong and powerful wings. It looked effortless. The old eagle watched with amazement at the bird. "Who's that?" he asked.*
>
> *"That's an eagle, king of the birds," said his neighbor. "He belongs to the sky. We belong to the ground."*
>
> *That is how an eagle was born and died like a chicken. Exactly what he believed and accepted was his whole life.*

As adults, we are not conscious of what our inner child still believes to be true. These false beliefs produce a person who fits the environment in which they were raised. Not being conscious of this causes many emotional problems, which lead us to fail in many different areas of our lives.

As humans, we have the right to have whatever our heart desires, unlimited prosperity, perfect health, beautiful relationships, and to live a life full of purpose. It is the right to live in the best and most beautiful way that you could possibly imagine, all in accordance with our highest dreams and aspirations.

To create a life, magnificent in all aspects, is possible when you let go of the false ideas that you have accepted about yourself, about life, and about people. To understand, to observe, and to be conscious of the fact that cycles repeat themselves will show you that your own parents were programmed by their own parents, most of the time in worst ways than they programmed you. Your life is a mirror, it shows you what you need to let go of subconsciously. Whatever it is that you need to let go of shows up through circumstances or experiences again and again, leaving a bitter taste. Whether that be in relation to your finances, your health, romantic relationship, or self-esteem.

The true power lies in taking the responsibility of loving and caring for your own inner child. You must understand the ideas, beliefs, and paradigms that the child accepted. Those that were imposed by society, religion, culture, and family. It is important to become conscious of how these beliefs are dominating control over your relationships, your health, your job, and your life. If you can achieve this, then you hold in your hands the option to truly enjoy being an adult who is conscious, creative, happy, and full of love for yourself as well as those around you.

We have been told that we are the architects of our own destiny. That we are the art as well as the artist. But who is the one who is creating? Psychologist Carl Jung said, "There is someone in my head, and it is not me." The answer is your inner child. This internal version of yourself who has been programmed with half-truths, and complete lies, which now govern your life. Have you ever asked yourself what the cause of your behavior is?

This book is written with the hope that it will help you find the answers to why you act the way that you do. Once you find the answers, you are then able to forgive others as well as yourself, let go of your fears, of your limiting beliefs, and live the life that you have always longed for but has always seemed out of reach.

Transform yourself into a Good Samaritan for your inner child since it has been abandoned, hurt, and left in the dust. Reconnect with them and help them heal their bruises. Feed them and assure them that no one will hurt them again. It is everyone's responsibility to remember who we truly are.

CHAPTER 1

Reconnecting With My Inner Child

> *"Our pain, our emotional wounds, are causing us to drift apart from each other."*
> *—Mercedes Guzman*

Joe Dispenza, a doctor in the field of biochemistry, said, "We are the creators of our own reality. The problem is that 95% of our subconscious thoughts create that reality. They are programs that function just under our consciousness, which memorize behaviors, thoughts, and emotional reactions. These programs are that which create the brain chemicals, which cause us to react to things in the same manner."

Personally, the idea that I was the cause of my pain was a concept that was so confusing, strange, and painful that I could not accept it very easily. How could it be possibly that I was the one creating so much pain? When I began to awaken to this new understanding, I saw that I created my reality of pain, anger, and fear. I would then use the techniques that I learned.

I meditated, prayed, and asked for guidance. However, I would find myself in the same cycles of pain just as before. Then I would get frustrated. I would cry, yell, and curse. But I had so much pain that it would just continue. There was no going back. In that pain, I had decided to push ahead, to understand myself, free myself from so much anxiety, fear, and anger. It did not matter what I felt, I pushed through and little by little I began to understand the process. It took me a long time to understand it, but looking back on the journey, it was all worth it.

It is my intention that, with this manual of my life, it does not take you as much time as it took me to understand that there was a forgotten little girl who felt abandoned, judged, and ignored and that she was the one who was determining my present experience.

I would like to add that you are not alone in this process. There is so much more help than you can possibly imagine: angels, spiritual guides, and a divine intelligence that can help you with everything. All you have to do is ask and be open to receiving guidance.

When you despair because things are not happening the way that you would like, talk to your inner child, which a lot of the time is the reason why you are feeling that despair. A child does not have a concept of time. They want everything that they want right now in that moment. Remember this in your own process.

The purpose of this book, through my own experiences, studies, as well as the studies of many experts, is to help you understand the origin of the beliefs that you accepted as a child. These beliefs come from your environment, circumstances, family, and religion. Growing up, you had no other choice. In the mind of a child, the adults have all of the answers.

To be clear, going back to your past and understanding your inner child DOES NOT mean going back to stay, nor to condemn your parents or the people that raised you. On the contrary, it is to go back to forgive and understand your aggressors. This process is not for them, it is completely for you. You must guide your inner child in a loving way back to its innocence and return to a state of love.

These beliefs about yourself, money, relationships, life, and death were all programmed into your subconscious. Once you understand the origins of these programs, of what happened to you on a conscious level, that understanding allows you to teach and show your inner child the different techniques that you have learned as an adult. Once you replace old, harmful programs with new healthy ones, you are able to let go and heal the mental patterns that have caused you so much pain and so many problems and insecurities. Then you are able to live the life that actually belongs to you from this new level of awareness.

How did I begin my journey of the inner child?

It all started around the year 1997 when we were living in Beaumont, Texas. My fourth child had just been born, and it was the first time that my parents were able to enter into the United States. They did not have their travel visas, so we had to apply for a resident's visa for them. This was how my parents came to be living with us, right before my beautiful son Gerson was born. At the time we lived in a three-bedroom apartment in a not-so-nice part of town.

I had gotten married to Daniel in El Salvador, my country of origin. Daniel is from Corpus Christi, Texas. He had come with a construction company to rebuild the American embassy, which had been destroyed by an earthquake in 1986. They were looking for an executive secretary, which was how the two of us met. He was my boss, a really great man, and was twenty-nine years old at the time. We fell in love, got married, and lived in El Salvador for a few years. It was in 1991 that we decided to move to the United States. By that time, I was already seven months pregnant with my first daughter, Yanica. I got to experience what it was like to be an immigrant although I came legally. I still experienced a lot of confusion from coming to live in a land completely different from my small little country. Without my family to turn to for help, I had to learn how to be a mother and housewife and learn to drive on huge roads, as well as learn a completely new language.

For two years, I lived in a state of depression, and my wish was to return to my country. I had one foot in the United States and the other in El Salvador, with strong feelings of instability, anxiety, and a lot of resentment.

It wasn't until one day I read a phrase that touched my soul, and I said to myself, "I have to change! I cannot go on like this." The phrase was "If you think that you have already lived the best parts of your life, then you have." I knew that there was still so much for me to do and experience, and it was then that I made the decision to focus on where I was and push forward. It was not easy, but when I commit to something, I give it my all.

By the time my parents came to the United States, a few years of learning and adapting had already passed. Three of my kids were already born, I had read lots of books, and I kept myself busy trying to do the best with everything that I had learned.

When my parents finally arrived, something very uncomfortable and frustrating happened. I felt strong feelings of anger and irritation towards my mother, which I unconsciously projected onto my children. When I did not know how to solve a problem or what to do with my little ones, I would grab them and punish them. I would become completely irrational, screaming, beating. I would become furious. Afterwards, I would feel guilty and really bad about my actions with desperation towards my behavior. I realized afterwards that this issue increased when my parents arrived. Although I had already been living with this cycle of pain before they came, it was not as apparent to me.

Afterwards, I would justify everything by saying that I was tired, that the kids would not listen, or that they were the problem. I would say that it was my nerves then blame my husband for not helping me or for not saying what he thought. At the time, the oldest of my children was only five years old.

> *"Observe your emotions: anger, sadness, guilt, shame, pain, jealously, hate, resentment. These hold the keys which open the memories that you lived day to day in your childhood and which are now repeated daily in your current life."*
> *—Mercedes Guzman*

I began to observe that when my mother would complain about my children, I would get very upset, and I would grab the child and spank them in front of her. Then I would yell at my mother and ask her if she was satisfied. The fury that I felt was illogical. It was like I was trying to punish my mother for something that I could not understand. This would just produce more blame, desperation, and anguish.

Because of this, I began to ask the universe for help. I remember that during that time, we were attending the Mormon Church, and there in silences, feeling like a failure with shame that made me feel like I was drowning, I asked God for help. By then I had come to hate myself for the pain that I had caused my children, my husband, myself, and my mother, but I did not know how to stop. It was as if something would seize control of me and would simply react, outside of my control.

My father had suffered from a mental illness and was left incapacitated. He would simply sleep, eat, use the bathroom, and my mother would take care of him. The father that I had been raised by had gone. That happy, compassionate, optimistic man had departed. The illness had shut down his mind. I simply felt pity and sadness for him.

The scriptures state, "Ask and it is given." I asked a lot of people if they knew anyone who could help me with my nervous problem. A friend from church referred me to a man named Juan de Dios. He was a Hispanic who did childhood regressions. This was a concept that really interested me, and I went to go see him.

Deep down, I knew that whatever was happening to me was psychological. What happened after those three sessions that I had with Juan de Dios was what changed my life. Because of the regressions that I had with him, I now help thousands of people around the world to heal their own inner child.

I got the information for Juan de Dios, and I was told that he received clients in his home. After talking to my husband about it, we decided to go and visit him. My husband and I arrived at his house which was a very tranquil and quiet environment. Juan was a very friendly man who made you feel at ease. We talked for a while about how he had gotten into doing what he did, and one thing that stood out to the both of us was his relaxed way at looking at life. He then led us to his office, which was on the main floor of his house. I remember our conversation going like this:

- Hello, Mercedes, how can I help you?

- I feel like it's my nerves. It's just that I get angry very easily with my children. I yell at them, I punish them, and I do not want to do it, but I do almost automatically. Afterwards, I feel terrible about myself.

- Let's take a look at what happened in your childhood in order to see what the cause of your stress in your life could be today. Close your eyes, take a few deep breaths, and take me back to the first image that you can remember of your mother.

- I am three years old. I am playing on the floor with my sister. My mom is standing with her back turned to me, looking at the street.

- Are you seeing the image in black and white or in color?

- In black and white.

This was the beginning of my reconnection with my inner child. The memories that came from my mind as a little girl were very sad. There was shouting, loneliness, beatings, fear, poverty. I remember my mother constantly telling me things, like how misbehaved I was, how I was a hypocrite, how I was a busybody, a liar, and how ungrateful I was. There were memories of being poor and looking at the furniture that we had, the clothes that we would wear. I remembered images of my mother constantly being sick, angry at my father and at life in general.

I had strong feelings of shame and guilt because when I was ten years old, I was sexually abused by a lady that my mom had given a job to. My mother would let her stay with us, and she would sleep in my bed with me, which was where she would touch me. In my mind, I was the one to blame for what had happened to me because of the sensations that I felt.

I never would have imagined that all of the craziness and desperation that was happening in the present had its origin in my childhood. It was very surreal, but it was happening, and it left me feeling weak, humiliated, angry, and completely disconnected.

Those regressions to my childhood made me realize that unconsciously, the one who was raising my children, reacting to them, screaming and hitting them, was the little ten- or fourteen-year-old girl in me that was holding onto all of those memories of pain and emotional trauma. Now that I was a mother myself and having to live under the same roof with my own mother after so many years of being apart, all of that pain and hurt that I was storing in my emotional body began coming out.

I returned to Juan de Dios two more times, and each visit left me surprised at how much my soul remembered and was able to heal in relation to what I had lived in my childhood.

Studies show that ninety percent of a child's brain develops before the age of six. These first years of life are essential in developing how the child thinks, feels, and acts in accordance to others.

Thurman Fleet created a drawing referred to as The Figure of The Mind in 1940 and said that the mind is divided in two parts: conscious and subconscious. Today, biologist Bruce Lipton ensures that neuroscience has proven that the conscious does not develop until six years old and that the minds of children before that age are on a frequency called theta, which is a hypnotic frequency. Therefore, a six-year-old does not have the ability to "analyze" that what is happening between mother and father is in fact having a huge impact on their life. They simply observe and store that information in the subconscious. Their mind is like a camera, simply capturing everything.

Back to the childhood

During the first five years of my life, a lot of things happened in my family. My parents were small merchants, which was what they called people who worked in the market. They had a mindset of poverty. Neither of them had attended school, and they had been raised by parents who had also not attended school. Without having an education and without being able to read or write very well, they struggled to provide for and sustain our family.

Studies by First Five LA show that kids who receive quality care as infants have higher levels of linguistic abilities, they perform better in school, and they have fewer behavioral problems and better social skills. During the first three years of my life, due to the poor mentality that my parents had and their own limitations, we lived in what was called mesons, or housing for the poor. In these places, it was very common for young people to sexually abuse small children like us who were around the ages of three and five.

My father, from the beginning of his marriage, began to drink and fight constantly with my mother. They fought to the point where my mother left when she was pregnant with her first child, who was born prematurely and died. The second time she left, she took my sister who was still a baby. Upon leaving, she went to her parents for help, but they refused to do anything. Being on her own, she decided to return to my father once again.

My mother had six kids, the first and the last child both died, however in four and a half years, she had the other four. Two daughters and two sons. I was the second born. Because of my parents' financial issues, which led to their inability to raise such a big family, they decided to go and live with my paternal grandmother, Grandma Maria, a woman raised in the country who could neither read nor write. She was widowed from my grandfather and never remarried. Due to her personality, she never liked my mother, and my mother made it very clear that she felt the same way about her. There was a lot of tension and anger between them in the beginning.

Towards the end of her life, my grandmother came to love my mom a lot, but in my first five years of living, the only thing that I remember feeling was just anger and irritation between the two.

My inner child and the prostitutes

My grandmother's house, where we went to live, was situated on the corner of a street where a lot of cars drove by, due to it being a busy business zone including a lot of brothels. My mother, who was raised by a family of merchants in the marketplace, saw an opportunity to open a small store in order to bring a source of income for the family. She decided to sell things like milk, bread, beans, rice, and candy.

The ladies of the happy life, as my grandmother would call the prostitutes, would come and buy from our little store. I remember my grandmother would grab a pole or a stick, and when they were not looking, would act like she was going to poke their butts, since they would wear such short dresses. I remember this very clearly, like it was yesterday. My little mind had so many questions. Who are these ladies? What do they do? Why do they wear so much makeup and wear such short dresses? Why does my grandmother make that sketchy smile when they come? I always wanted to go into one of the houses and see what was going on. I have always been curious, so curious, and at five years old, I was no different.

In most eras of human existence, it is considered that those who take up work as prostitutes are lowlifes and the subject is taboo, denying or covering up their existence. There is no research nor attempt to understand why they lived the way that they do or work in their chosen profession. It is better to simply avoid the topic because it is considered something vulgar, causing it to be maintained in secret. What is interesting is that this happens all of the time. If people were really educated and informed about this world in which a lot of women live, they would be more compassionate. They have inner children who have been programmed, abused, and most don't see any other option of making money, therefore they choose this life.

My family, however, was no different, even living amongst them. This was a marginal topic in many conversations, but their beliefs and paradigms over the lives of these women was something that was on the mind of the adults, and for a lot of the men, visiting these brothels was a part of their hidden lives. At my five years of age, I did not understand what went on in these places, but I assumed that it was something very strange that no one could talk about clearly. Only through whispers.

My inner child and exclusion

Also living in my grandmother's house were a few of my cousins, children of my father's half-brother. Some were older young adults, so in total, there were around ten people living in a four-bedroom house with one bathroom. You can imagine the feeling of being left out in an environment like this. Living in a place that was not our home, this is where I accepted the subconscious belief that I do not belong. This is a feeling that is very common in the lives of most people, yet very few take the time to stop and ask themselves where that feeling is stemming from or where exactly they picked it up.

> *"Most of the time, the thing that counts is not necessarily what happened to you but how your inner child interpreted what was happening."* —Mercedes Guzman

One of the primary memories that I have at that time was that at five years old, my sister and I wanted to run away from home. I remember hiding a cardboard box under the dresser, and I told myself that it was where we were going to pack our clothes and take the box with us when we finally decided to go.

I have asked my sister if she remembers that situation, but she said that she does not. However, my mother told me a story that when my sister was only four years old, she took me by the hand and walked a few blocks through crowded streets, and we ended up at my grandmother's house. I was three years old at the time. That shows me the level of stress that there was in living in that house and how we wished to escape from it by running away. I know that it was real for me and that it really happened, because I did the same thing unconsciously to my own children. There were times when I shouted things to my five- and six-year-old such as, "Leave then! If you don't want to listen to me. Leave and see who would want you. I'll take you to a family that will finish raising you!" If this had not been implanted in my childhood, these would be very difficult things to say to my own children, and things like this would come up in me all the time.

Something similar or worse had to have happened. Being a child and not understanding the concept, what you do is save these memories, and eventually they have to reemerge at some point in your life. Sadly, the moment that these manifest is with your own children or with your spouse.

> *"The subconscious tends to repeat experiences in your adult life that are very similar to events in your childhood that caused emotional pains."* —Mercedes Guzman

For some reason, there is a memory in which I am sitting at the table with my siblings, and with the mindset of a little girl, I remember thinking very clearly, "The adults in this house want to poison us." What I felt was that we were a nuisance to them and that they did not want us because we bothered them. I now know that the feeling was coming from the insecurity that my mother felt living in a house that did not belong to her, and having so many little kids, in ignorance of how to improve the situation. That insecurity would be vocalized in punishing and mistreating her children. Additionally, my grandmother would also scold us with rage and ignorance. A little child cannot understand this and simply stores the feelings and memories away.

I would like to say that there were a few good memories during that time, and it is very important to hold onto those. But I have understood throughout my studies that the most important thing to do is to release the painful memories. It is not until you do so that you can begin to live a life full of peace. The pain of those memories blocks out all of the nice things that happened.

My inner child and her father

Two months before getting married to my mother, my father was taken by the national guard of our country. They were accusing him of stealing cows, which was not true. He was very severely tortured by these men and was suffocated in order to try to get him to confess.

My father's brothers were able to rescue him from this organization that violated every human right possible. After that tragedy, his mind was never clear. We think that this event triggered the beginning of his later schizophrenia.

The fact that my mother did not quite understand what was going on with my father caused a lot of issues between them and resulted in lots of fights. My father would try making money in many ways to end up simply borrowing money. Someone lent him money to buy a pig. I remember the morning they killed the pig on my grandmother's patio and took the meat to go sell it at the market. I also remember the feelings that no matter what my father did, the money never lasted, and my mother was always mad at him for that.

When they would kill those pigs at the house, you could hear really strange sounds. One morning I woke up, and I went to go watch. The general feeling of the situation was something that I can now explain as "This is illegal. Do not tell anyone."

> *"There is a belief that you do not have to explain to children what is going on, because it is assumed that they do not understand. This is completely false."*
> —Mercedes Guzman

Sometimes they would wake us up early and take us to a place called Hogar del Nino—house of kids. It was a place for children of low-income families. They would leave us here for the majority of the day. I remember not wanting to go. I would cry a lot, but once we got there, we were greeted by a very nice lady named Juanita. The smell and the taste of beans and scrambled eggs for breakfast was something that stuck with me, since they were always very delicious.

They would teach us a few things, and then have us take naps on the floor with the other kids. A lot of the time we would get contaminated with lice, and they would have to give us medicine to kill them. At this place, my father learned that we could start kindergarten in one of the best Catholic schools in the area, as they had decided to accept underprivileged kids as a service to the community.

My inner child and religion

During the time that we were living with my grandmother, I learned to fear God. It seemed like every admonishment was "GOD WILL PUNISH YOU!" As my grandmother did not trust anyone, I also, as an adult, began to do the same. I would not leave my purse anywhere or with anyone. I was always scared that someone was going to steal it. I now understand where that programming came from.

My grandmother had an altar with all of the saints, which she worshiped, and if she ever lost anything, she would get down on her knees and in a loud voice ask Saint Anthony to help her find what she had lost. A lot of the time you would hear her shouting with joy and thanking Saint Anthony for finding the comb that someone had stolen or that she had misplaced. Because of this, I developed the belief in a higher power that would either help you or punish you, depending on how you acted.

The paradigm of religion is learned by the child in the first year of life. If the parents are Catholic, Pentecostal, Mormon, Jewish, or Muslim, this will typically be the religion that the child will follow once they reach adulthood. And even if consciously they do not feel like it is the right religion for them and they want to separate themselves from their parents' beliefs, they typically experience a lot of anxiety because of the feeling of guilt for having abandoned an idea which was implanted into their subconscious at such an early age. This makes it very difficult for the adult to remove themselves from the religion of their parents. This is why many resort to questionable living, addictions, and other vices, performing self-destructive acts when they "leave the chosen path."

My inner child and Santa Claus

When I was five years old, I realized that Santa Clause was a bad guy, seeing as I would act nicely, and he still would never leave me anything good for Christmas. I remember one Christmas Eve in particular, I had asked one of my cousins, who was fifteen, to help me write a letter to Santa. In the letter I asked for a beautiful doll with a dress and a boyfriend for her. The next day, what I found was a plastic doll whose eyes didn't even move. It was all my cousin could buy with a few cents so that at least I would have something. In my mind, as a little girl, I did not understand that it was my cousin who had gotten me the doll. I simply believed that I had done something wrong, and that was why Santa had not brought me what I had asked for. After that, I became rebellious and started misbehaving.

My inner child and death

At the age of five, I learned about death in a way that was very sad and tragic. The first death was the last child my mother had. My mother was left in the hospital, while my father brought the dead child to his mother's house, where they had a very small ceremony then went to the cemetery and buried her. We were all very young, and no one explained to us what had happened.

The second death was when the war in my country had started, and there were battles between the guerrilla rebels and the government military. I remember very clearly that, one morning, a man who frequented the brothel next to our grandmother's home was found dead in front of the brothel. Due to lack of education, the adults did not think that the children understood anything, and so they never explained what was going on. Everything that you see must be given some sort of meaning. I still only have the image of a group of people, gathering around to see the dead guy, and that is it.

It left a lot of questions: What happens afterwards? Where does the body go? Where does the soul go? None of these questions were answered. The adults would just tell us stories to scare us in order to calm us down if we were crying. For example, they would tell us, "Be quiet or the dead will come and take you away." Or "Be quiet or the cat will come and eat your tongue." Or we would hear legends of The Witch Wagon or El Cipitio.

During that same time, a kid who was around our age was crossing the road and got struck by a car. My mother started screaming at the top of her lungs and needed to be calmed down. She thought that it was one of us who had gotten killed. Again, no one explained to me what was going on, and I was left traumatized by seeing how life can be taken away in an instant.

My inner child and guilt and shame

When I was six years old, doctors found out that I had an inguinal hernia. The surgery to get it removed took place in a hospital for people of lower income. I remember the nurses were more kind to me than the rest of the kids since I had blonde hair and green eyes. I learned that things are not equal for everyone. They let me go after two weeks, and I was unable to walk. I remember my father carrying me in his arms and climbing onto a bus, since he never learned how to drive nor did he own a vehicle. I was embarrassed for people to see me being carried by my father. It did not seem right because I felt guilt and thought I was grown up, and people should not have to do things like that for me. This is a common sentiment for children, and that is the feeling of not deserving.

My grandmother was really happy to see me when we got home. After a short time, I remember fighting a lot with her. This was because I was always questioning their behavior and she tried to punish me for that.

I also have memories of scratching one of my classmates for no reason. Now I understand that I became aggressive because of all the anger that I lived with in my home. Not understanding what was happening was made manifest in aggression towards others. I also started receiving more frequent beatings from my mother. I would not let her grab me, and that would just frustrate her even more. Knowing that she could not control me, she would hit and punish me harder.

> *"The emotional pain of a child, leads to an aggressive child or a shy child." —Mercedes Guzman*

My inner child and witches

During this time, I learned that "there are witches that do harm to others," or at least that's what everyone would say, but no one would really explain it. They would just mention that there was this woman named Old Aida and that she had cursed us. We began to live with a ghost in the house.

I learned years later that this lady had done some "evil" to our house, and that was why we would hear noises at night. The doors would slam, footsteps would be heard, and apparently there were lights that could be seen here and there. Within the household, it was a time of a lot of fear. Once again, the adults would not explain anything to us because they thought that we did not understand, although to be fair, they did not quite know what was going on either. This situation created in me the feeling that others can do you harm, that others were to blame for your problems. You have no control over it nor can you avoid it. When we would cry out of fear, the adults would increment our fears, tell us to be quiet or the witch wagon would come and take us away.

There are studies that show when a child does not understand what is happening in their home, they store everything in their emotional body. This is how all of that fear gets caught and stays trapped in the inner child. It produces a fear without basis which is rooted in certain experiences, creating an adult who is ignorant where their own paranoias, fears, and insecurities come from.

My parents were tired of living with my grandmother but were unable to move. This was when my grandmother decided to sell her house. My father decided that it would be better for us to find our own place to live. With a little bit of money that my grandmother gave to my parents from helping her sell the house, they were able to buy a small house that was far away from my grandmother's new place. With very few things, we went to go live in this very humble home that consisted of two bedrooms, one bathroom, a kitchen, and a small living room.

By that time, my siblings and I had already begun attending a Catholic school name Escuela Santa Sofia. It meant that we would now receive a higher quality education.

CHAPTER 2

The Subconscious Mind – Inner Child

> *"There is a common mind which exists in each and every human."* —Ralph W. Emerson

The kahunas, or Hawaiian priests, believe that the basic I, or the inner child, is the holding place of all memories, what you would call the subconscious mind.

What is the subconscious mind? It is the part of your mind which has received orders and acts automatically, without thought and in general not depending on will power. If it is programmed in a negative way, it can lead to actions that can be harmful or dangerous without taking into account the risks or consequences. This is where all of your paradigms and a gambit of beliefs were accepted by your inner child. This creates a borrowed life. You do not live your true life, since the majority of it is simply cycles that you are unconsciously carrying around from your parents, grandparents, or family that you were raised by.

The psychologist D.W. Winnicott said that in our childhood, "things happened that should not have happened, and many things that should have happened did not." The first of these things is the abuses, abandonments, and all kinds of secrets that were given. The second is the kids that were not abused were given food and a home, but a loving parent was not present due to stress and societal demands. This is called proximate abandonment.

At Harvard University, violent people have been studied, and it has been proven that the most violent were victims of things in their childhood in such a harsh way that you cannot put into words the struggle that they went through. This leads to the conclusion that violence is not inherited, it is learned. Your heart and your mind hold this information.

Rollin McCraty, director of the Heart Math Institute said, "Consider the incredible human heart. This organ which constantly pumps oxygen and nutrient rich blood all over our bodies. Now studies are finding that this marvelous machine, the size of a fist, and that weighs less that ten ounces, possesses a level of intelligence which we are just now starting to understand. Evidence shows that the heart plays a bigger part in our mental, emotional, and physical processes than we previously thought." He records that "the heart is a sensory organ which acts as a sophisticated coding mechanism and a processing center which allows it to learn, store information, and take functional decision independently."

My question is: On what basis of programming is the heart acting like an information encoder? In reality, it is our inner child that is determining this information, since the primary memories are saved in the amygdala, which forms part of what is called the deep brain. That is where you find the basic emotions like rage and fear and also the will to survive. This is also found in the depths of the temporal lobes, forming the limbic system and processing everything relative to our emotional reactions. This is responsible for helping us escape dangerous situations, but it is also responsible for recording and holding onto those traumatic experiences as children and anything that caused us to suffer at some point.

The physician Gabor Maté expressed there are studies done which show that children who were adopted at birth, even when they are not told that they were adopted, and were raised by very loving parents, still exhibit behaviors and feelings of abandonment and rejection when they grow older. The memories that the child experiences stay saved in the subconscious mind and these reproduce themselves in the form of bad characters, social problems, low self-esteem, illness, financial issues, and relationship issues.

The same studies mention that it is extremely important to the mental development of a child to hold them. This is opposite to what many believe, as many of us were left in our cribs to cry because it was thought that you would raise a spoiled child if you picked them up when they cried. This is the opposite of what should be done to a child. All of these memories of abandonment and rejection are collected and held in what is called the implicit memory, or emotional body.

Life is governed by laws and principles

Favoritism does not exist in this universe. Life is not a question of predestination or bad luck. The key to success in all humans lies in their own thinking, which relies on an infallible law: the law of cause and effect.

Thought is the origin of feeling, and feeling creates our emotions, and our emotions create our reality. The law of cause and effect always works and does not play favorites. When a child has been negatively programmed, they grow into an adult with issues in certain areas of their lives because of this law. The life that we create from this programming is typically an experience of pain, poverty, low self-esteem, or traumatic relationships. All of it is driven by the subconscious mind or your inner child.

After the regressions that I had with Juan de Dios, I gave myself the task of studying the mind. My husband signed me up for a book club, which would send me one book a month. I began to study books on psychology, meditation, personal growth, and different spiritual paths. One of my daily prayers was, "Divine presence, send me the books that I need to read in order to acquire the knowledge that exists but that I do not know it exists."

Wayne Dyer and Deepak Chopra were two of the authors that first appeared in my life. I began to read their books all the time. These helped me to begin to awaken as an adult, and the explanations that I would read in these books would give me a clear idea of how the mind worked, and they gave me the techniques I needed in order to free myself from the accumulated pain that I was still holding on to. Even with these studies, my inner child was not something that was a priority in my life. It was not until a few years later that I started being the Good Samaritan and took the responsibility of caring for my inner child. This began to heal my emotional injuries on a deeper level.

One after another, the books began to reveal themselves to me. A lot of the time, they seemed to jump out at me from book stands, or sometimes they would come to me through someone else, while some I would find through what seemed like miracles. I was so thirsty for knowledge that I would read until I was exhausted. One of the books that really opened my eyes in a big way was *Basic Principles of the Science of Mind* by Frederik Bailes. This book gave me a lot of the basis in which I began using the power of thought in order to physically heal myself as well as my children. Because of what I learned from this book and through applying it in my life, I have managed to not go to any doctors for over twenty-four years now, and I also managed to avoid taking my children to any sort of doctors as well. This, however, is my own personal experience, and I would like to say that I am not suggesting that you do the same, or that doctors do not know what they are doing.

Through all of these studies, I slowly began to become aware of the fact that someone who was not 'me' was making decisions automatically and preventing me from acting in the way that I consciously wished that I could act. My biggest wish was to be a good mother, good wife, good daughter. Nonetheless, I felt like I was failing in all areas of my life.

Step by step, and with a lot of patience, I kept reading, hoping to find some magic pill that would heal my craziness. But I had to go through a lot of trial and error, studies and applications, before I realized completely that the journey had only just begun and that I was not alone, because it was my inner child who needed my love.

CHAPTER 3

My Inner Child at Seven Years Old

By the time I turned seven, things were getting better. Moving to a house of our own was the beginning of a better life. My neighbor had a daughter who went to the same school that I went to, and she was my same age.

Now that we were living in a neighborhood, we lived on a street called Los Laureles, which was a small road where cars did not pass through, allowing us to safely play outside. This was something that we could not do when we lived at my grandmother's house.

Daily, my parents had to go to work at the market, which meant that we had to wake up early and walk with my mother to school. The starting time was 7:30 a.m., and we had to be on time. If not, they would make us stand on the patio for half an hour with the sun beaming down on us. The trip to school would take about thirty minutes, and for the most part, we were walking on dirt. We would bring a brush to clean off our shoes, because our school had very strict rules about having clean shoes.

At 12:30, once school had ended, the next step was to walk back to the market to help my mom with her business of selling food. At work, we would wash dishes and clean. We would be done around four in the afternoon. Then we would walk back to our house to do some chores, after which we would get a chance to play for a while. The routine was the same, day after day.

I loved school. It was a really clean place with wonderful teachers. Because I talked too much, I was always in trouble or on the naughty list. What caused me anguish was that I had already accepted that I was misbehaved or would ask too many questions. Now that I give conferences and am a coach, I realize that my ability to talk so much was actually one of my gifts, but it just always seemed to bother the teachers, since I would ask so many questions that sometimes they did not know the answer to.

At the age of seven, the child begins to show what they had learned within their first five years. If the child accepts that they do not deserve anything, they will begin to attract teachers and classmates who reinforce that idea. For example, if a mother brings a cake to school to celebrate her child's birthday, when it comes your turn to receive a slice, they run out of cake. The child who has that sort of programming will tell themselves, "I did not deserve the cake," and they assume that it was their fault for not having received any. A child who does not have that programing would look at the same situation and accept the fact that they just ran out of cake, without taking it personally.

Bruce Lipton, a renowned biologist, explains how science reveals the brain receives orders through thoughts and feelings. These thoughts and feelings are 95% influenced by our subconscious mind, which is governed by all of the programming and false beliefs that we have picked up throughout our lives. Then human beings only act with 5% consciousness unaffected by preprogramming. This is where our adult tasks are: lose weight, find a partner, be a better mother or a better student, write a book, be a better daughter. But in the end, they do not end up being accomplished, and the cycle of frustration simply gets worse each time.

Without noticing, our inner child takes control, and it is for that reason that we are left thinking things like, "Why did I say that when I really did not want to say it?" or "Why did I do that again when I had promised myself that I would not do it again?" This is the category for all those individuals that promised "never to do that again," leading many to addictions, such as alcohol, drugs, sex, or food, even when they know that they are risking losing their families, jobs, and relationships.

The reason is that, without us noticing, all of our programming that we accepted in our childhood is what is determining the important decisions in our lives. Some state that the wounded inner child unites with your ego, or shadow. This is why we sometimes see pastors, government officials, or schoolteachers who publicly condemn homosexuality, cheating, and sexual abuse of children yet are later seen on the news for doing the exact same thing that they were condemning.

Without knowing, we repeat cycles until we get sick of being sick. Then we start to heal those emotional wounds that have been left open. Neuroscience shows how the brains of children under six years have not developed a conscience. This resides in the frontal region of the brain. The brain wave frequency in those first years is what is referred to as theta, which is a hypnotic state. What that implies is that everything is saved in the subconscious without the child able to do anything about it.

A child that young cannot make sense or understand, since their brain does not have conscious capacity, as it is still developing. The child, therefore, unable to understand the reason for their pain, simply stores the memories, forgetting what happened.

Quantum physics tells us that our thoughts are energy, and we know that energy cannot be destroyed, only transformed. What we experience as children does not disappear, it is stored and eventually has to be released. We have been taught to grow to become responsible adults, and many of us believe that we have reached that point. We adopt positions of power as executives, politicians, actors, singers, doctors, and ecclesiastical figures who hold a lot of influence through responses and large corporations. Studying their lives, we see kids who are traumatized, tyrants, controllers, abusers, and sex, food, and drug addicts who pretend to have control of their life but are broken inside. Without being aware of that fact, they inflict and project that pain onto others, especially the ones who they love.

One of the most extreme cases of this is that of Hitler. His childhood was painful and took place in the midst of a hard-authoritarian father named Alois. He was a well-to-do customs agent who was cruel and violent. The pain and trauma Hitler experienced in his childhood led him to be responsible for the death of millions. It is unimaginable trying to recount all the harm and indescribable things that this man did due to his wounded inner child.

My mother had a very hard childhood. When my grandmother got pregnant, her husband accused her of infidelity, and he humiliated her a lot of different times. When my mother was finally born, my grandfather did not accept her as his child, so he did not show her any love or affection. Later on, my grandfather realized that my mother had a lot of things in common with him, like birthmarks, gestures, and her ears and legs even resembled his.

There were eight people in my mother's family, and they were raised in extreme poverty. My grandfather was a tyrant. He would hit them and intimidate them. My grandmother would not interfere because of fear. Neither of my grandparents had the opportunity to go to school, since their own parents did not believe in it. However, my grandfather was very intelligent, and he taught himself how to read and write. Then he would teach his own kids with violence and cruelty when they did not understand what he meant.

My mother, who took a lot of the abuse from her father, was the fifth child. This was a cycle that repeated itself when she got married and had four children, who later turned into five when she adopted a ten-year-old little girl. This little girl was a friend of ours from the neighborhood whose mother moved to a place without water or electricity. Upon seeing her in that situation, my sister and I begged our mother to let her live with us. Due to our pleading, my mother eventually agreed, and after speaking to the girl's mother, Daisy came to live with us. This was when I was nine, and to this day we still consider each other loving sisters.

Patterns of behavior created to survive

In order to continue to live in a world that does not make sense, children typically create patterns of behavior that help them to cover up, or to survive, the pain that they live. Examples of this are kids that laugh all of the time, even when they are being punished or made fun of. Many refer to these children as clowns, oftentimes even their own parents or their caretakers. Other children begin to lie constantly, some forget things easily. Some steal, some become like tyrants, and then some make themselves constantly sick. The children with the major problems and issues become submissive. These are more apt to be noticed by sexual predators, victimizers, and are the ones singled out by some schoolteachers to scold and mistreat the most.

CHAPTER 4

Loss of Memory and Your Inner Child

One of the things that happened between the ages of five and ten was that I began using a defense mechanism. I began to forget certain situations. From one year to the next, I began forgetting who had been in my class the year before, or I would never hold grudges because I would forget who had been mean to me. People said I forgave very easily because of this. If an adult is not conscious of this, they may begin to say, "I always forget everything! I am losing my memory." Sometimes they do not realize that this also happened when they were young. Without knowing it, they continue to program their subconscious in this manner, and eventually these people suffer from dementia or Alzheimer's. The subconscious does not question, it simply receives orders. Who is giving these orders? It is a wounded inner child.

Unconsciously I had accepted the fact that I was going to go crazy, due to the fact that when I was nine, my grandmother lost her mind and reverted back to acting like a little girl who was looking for her mother. My father then followed the cycle of his mother by also exhibiting the same loss of mental focus. As I worked restoring my inner child, I realized that this was something that I had accepted, and with the power of my own intention and conscious thought, I canceled this order that I had given my subconscious mind.

A child, by not understanding their environment, thinks that they are responsible for the ignorance with which they are raised. The child begins to feel very angry on the inside, and without being able to express that anger, their self-esteem begins to drop and has the ability to reach levels that are so low, it may cause the child to run away or even kill themselves.

In my case, I remember mentally insulting my mother and feeling a great deal of rage towards the unfair punishments that they would inflict on us. I reached a point where I would not cry anymore when they would punish me. I would stand firm and promise myself that I would not cry. I would repeat to myself, "Hit me, but I will not cry!" It was my own way of punishing my mother, by not letting her see me cry. Then I would either return to my room or go back to doing whatever it was that they would ask of me. However, I would do it with a very sad, hopeless attitude.

This behavior of "not feeling," blocks good feelings like joy as well. It is like putting anesthesia on the heart. That is why many people walk with a hunch on their back, because they began to close their hearts when they were young, and they desperately carry their pain around with them as if on their backs. When the mind feels a certain way, it causes the body to respond in like manner.

My father, on the contrary, was a very calm man, and he did not like to hit us very often, but my mother would tell him to hit us anyway. He had suffered a lot of beatings from his own mother, and he did not want to do the same to us, but he did not know how to close the cycle. He was an obedient child, and so he had to continue this cycle as an adult, as he married my mother, who always saw him as someone who did not provide and therefore would punish him emotionally for this. Because of the shame he felt as a child for not having done things right, he perpetuated the cycle of "I am not enough, I don't deserve, punishment me."

CHAPTER 5

To Bless or Condemn and Your Inner Child

The belief that many parents have towards raising their children adds more conflicts. Thousands of parents never stop to ask:

Why do I always think that my child is going to get sick?

Why am I always thinking about sickness?

Why do I worry and only think that the worst is going to happen?

Why do I react this way with my children, especially when I do not want to?

Why do I say no all the time?

Why do I remain angry, frustrated, or ill?

Parents unknowingly pass down the same chains that they received from their parents. This is transmitted through solitude, abandonment, verbal and physical abuse, and not being considerate. They raise programmed children then blame these children when they get into trouble. Without knowing, these parents, by their unconsciousness, focus on problems, complain, curse, and use the creative power of the mind to create the worst. Parents are always thinking that something bad will happen to their children. Then when the child does not obey them, in their desperation, they may think or verbalize something terrible such as telling their kid that they are going to end up in prison or worse. When this happens, the adult unconsciously sends that child to prison in their mind or pictures them having some harsh accident, and it is through this power of the mind, the child is pushed towards the direction of those real-world events and only perpetuate this cycle of pain.

I had a client come visit me whose life had become a martyrdom in all aspects. When we went back to visit her inner child, she was the only girl among four brothers, and she remembered one night when she was eight years old, hearing her mother yell at her father and say, "Your daughter will be dammed because of what you have done to me!" Then her mother became very stern with her because of her father's infidelity. This event was hidden in her subconscious, repressed and forgotten.

However, silently, this little girl accepted that bad things would happen in her life because of those words from her mother. In a very beautiful way, I was able to help her release this memory, heal this point in her life, and was able to tell her that it was not her fault and that the things that her mother had said had nothing to do with her.

Since that session, she has told me that she has continued talking to her inner child, showing her and teaching her the things that she now knows as an adult. She said that she feels so much more at peace, and she is seeing and living positive results in her life.

We also see young people looking for motherly or fatherly love and affection, seeking in their partners what they did not get from their parents. They attempt to find this love through sex, and since they cannot receive what they needed as children, they fall into cycles of abandonment, or abuse, which causes even more pain and trauma. If this pain gets too big and unbearable, they turn to drugs or alcohol and only repeat the cycle with their own children.

The mind has the power to create health or sickness, just like it can create happiness or sadness, riches or poverty. Without understanding this power that each and every human possesses, what we achieve is the unconscious passing down of the same patterns from generation to generation. Let us not forget or ignore the beautiful things that happen during the lives of people as they are raised. We must also understand that everything that has happened has played a part in making you who you are today. However, you cannot truly heal unless you pass through the pain, understand it, heal it, then let it go.

Understanding what happened in your childhood gives you that opportunity, a chance to give your inner child a voice and to tell that child inside that whatever happened was not their fault nor their responsibility. In doing this, you learn to love that part of yourself once again, and you prevent it from continuing to hold you back from progressing in the different areas of your life.

CHAPTER 6

It Was Not Your Fault, It Never Was

> *When I was a child, I spoke like a child. I understood like a child, I thought like a child. I played like a child. When I became a man, I set aside childish things.*
> *—1 Corinthians 13:11*
>
> *"Blame represents death in the exact way that love represents life. Blame is part of the smallest self and underlies our will to believe in negative things about ourselves."*
> *—Dr. David Hawkins*

What is it that makes me feel so guilty if I have done nothing to feel guilty about? This is a question that we will explore!

There were many Saturdays and Sundays that my mother did not want to take my siblings and I all to the marketplace because caring for young children in the market environment was more work for her than the work she could get out of the four of us. The most convenient thing to do was to leave us in the house and lock it up. I was the second born, and I was around eight years old when this began to happen. My mother would assign us different chores to do like sweeping, mopping, washing dishes, or washing clothes. Being kids, these were the last things that we wanted to do, and we would use most of our time to find trouble to get into.

During that time, there was no television or phone in the house. My hometown of San Miguel is a place that is very hot, and so I would sleep a lot. I remember sometimes I would sleep, and I would want to wake up, but I could not and felt like my body was floating. It is a very faint memory, like it's a part of my thoughts that my mind erased.

Being creative kids, we would get curious as to how we could escape from the house. We would climb walls and even get on the roof. Then one day, we figured out how to open the front door. We would play in the streets and explore, and when we knew that our parents would be back, we would lock the door again and pretend like nothing had happened. We would not do a very good job with the chores, and a lot of the times we would just forget to do them. My mother would get back home, tired and stressed out, and as usual this would give her a reason to scold and spank us.

Children do not understand adults, and they just assume that they do not make mistakes. I had growing feelings of shame and guilt. First for not obeying, but also because we would hide the fact that we had learned how to escape from the house without them knowing. The day my parents finally found out that we were escaping, they were very upset, and the punishment was severe. Even though it is against the law to leave your children alone, the idea that was programmed into me was "It is all my fault." I blamed myself for not being better, and part of me believed that I deserved the punishment.

As my tenth year was passing, I remember feelings of sadness and self-rejection. Also, I felt a lot of guilt. The majority of children that age begin to create their own beliefs around money, relationships, and health. They feel contempt towards themselves, and this is when many decide to push ahead, but they do it from a place of pain and fear. Then they may reach great heights in life, but it is their emotional lives that really affects them. We can see these effects in great singers who destroy themselves, such as Whitney Houston, Michael Jackson, and Elvis Presley, to name a few.

This was a period in which my mother would help the kids who were worse off than we were. She would let them live in our house, and in exchange, they would help her out in the market. Because there was not much space, she would assign them to either sleep with me or my sister. This was where one of the young girls would touch me at night.

I remember that I would stay silent because my body began to feel things that I did not understand, and I would keep it a secret out of shame. I thought that it was my fault that it had happened because I had begun to feel those sensations that I was not used to. More and more guilt was growing in my subconscious.

What is guilt? Many authors define guilt as a painful effect that surges from the belief or feeling of having overstepped personal or social norms, especially if you have hurt someone in the process. A child does not understand that it is not their fault when they answer in a rude way or they do things that are considered improper.

They simply reflect that which their parents or caretakers have shown them over time. So the only one to blame is the ignorance and unconsciousness of the subject. It is a cycle that is very difficult to get out of since it comes from generation to generation, and we cannot sit and blame our parents or those who raised us, since they are programmed in the same manner or worse. It is like asking the question of whether the chicken or the egg came first.

In my experience, I have come to realize that children, or let's say you, in your childhood, confused guilt with shame, causing even more emotional pain since guilt and shame create the perfect conditions for self-destruction. This is where depression starts and a whole spectrum of emotional problems arise.

Guilt appears before the supposed pain for the wrong done. Shame is experienced when we accept, with the limited knowledge that we have acquired at our young age, that it is our fault for not having developed abilities or skills that are expected of us at that age. A clear example of this is when a child spills milk or juice and their parents make this event bigger than it really is, causing the child to believe that they are clumsy. This can be very damaging when a child is only just learning how to really use their motor skills and they make small mistakes.

In his book, *Letting go the Pathway of Surrender*, Dr. David Hawkins talked about guilt in this manner:

> *One particular form of fear is what we call guilt. Guilt is always associated with a sensation of injustice and potential punishment, whether that be real or fantasy. If the punishment is not received in the physical world, it is experienced as self-punishment at an emotional level. Guilt accompanies all of the negative emotions and because of that, where there is fear, there is guilt. If you think a guilty thought and you have someone test your strength, you will see that the muscles go weak instantly. Your cerebral hemispheres desynchronize, and all of your energy centers become uncalibrated. Nature then tells us that guilt is destructive.*

You are not what you think you are, it is not your fault. On being born, you enter a world that is already programmed and conditioned by the prejudices and ignorance of our ancestors. At the point of your birth, you are already the sum of everything that you heard while you were in the womb. There you were, present and assimilating the conversations that were being held between your parents, your grandparents, and whomever else. On top of that, you would experience the emotions of guilt, fear, and sadness that your mother would experience.

You are born, and they begin to fill your head with phrases like, "Careful, you're going to fall," "No," "Don't talk back to me, you misbehaved little one," "Put your shoes on, you'll catch a cold," "If you keep crying, I'm going to hit you," "There are bad people, don't trust strangers," "Get an education so you can graduate and live well," "There is not enough money. Do you think it grows on trees?" etc., etc., etc.

You grow up being afraid of a whole conglomerate of ideas, and being so young, without your frontal lobe being developed enough to allow you to decide things for yourself, you become someone that you are not. You mind becomes filled with voices telling you things that you think are you, but in reality, they were someone else's ideas, fears, and insecurities.

I remember a client of mine who, at the age of sixty-two, remembered a phrase that her mother would tell her when she did not want to eat anymore. "Eat everything on your plate because there are kids dying of hunger and you are sitting here, ungrateful." She told me that even to this day, she has trouble not eating everything on her plate, even when she is full, because she feels so guilty. This has led her to become overweight, and when she knows that she should stop eating, she continues. In speaking with her, she realized that it was not a personal belief, but one that was planted there by her mother and was probably planted into her mother by her grandmother.

Dr. Hawkins reaffirms that "99% of the time, guilt does not have anything to do with reality. In fact, the people who are the most pious, gentle, and simple are oftentimes filled with guilt."

We were taught to feel guilty, scared, and anxious. The word educate comes from the Latin *ex ducere* which means "to take from inside." Take from where and to take what, though? One thing that many fail to learn in school is that everything that you need to know is already inside of yourself. If you learn to study your being, you begin to realize that everything that you wish already is. You simply have to ask, then silence yourself, and from the depths of your being you will pull out that which you favor. Values, love, peace, virtues, willpower, self-domination, generosity, and all else. How wonderful it would be if they taught us this in school, but unfortunately most of what school teaches simply fills our minds with dates, information, and guilt. This is not sufficient to raise healthy adults.

Accepting all of this without questioning has made a lot of people lose the taste for life. In reference to education, many are told, "Study and you will get a good job." And now we see streets filled with educated people with degrees but still without work, or with a job but with an overwhelming feeling of emptiness. With this, I am not saying that secular studies have no benefit. On the contrary, they enrich your life. But the study of self takes you to new levels of awareness and of being.

Dr. Hawkins talks about the effects of guilt and how it makes us feel:

> *Guilt is as frequent as fear, and we end up feeling guilty without understanding what we are doing. One part of our mind tells us that in reality, we should be doing something else. Or, what we are really doing in this moment, we should be doing it better. We "should" be getting a better score in golf. We "should" be reading a book instead of watching TV. We "should" be making love better. Cooking better. Running faster. Grow taller. Be stronger. Be more intelligent. Be more educated. In between the fear of life and the fear of death is the guilt of the moment. We try to escape the guilt while remaining unconscious to it through suppression, repression, projection onto others, and escaping.*

Humanity is waking up and many are beginning to feel tired of the same beliefs and are now asking themselves different questions, which can be heard by listening to youths. *How is this information going to help me? Why do we have to study this?* A new consciousness is coming about every day, and more and more people are coming to understand that we are beings with unlimited potential and power and that we have the capabilities to create favorable situations by simply changing our thoughts and releasing guilt and blame. These processes change our attitude, which in turn changes our actions, and if we keep applying this concept, we are able to change the direction of our lives, and the feeling of guilt begins to dissipate.

It is because of this that we have to observe our own guilt, since it is always present, and if we do not become aware of it, this feeling governs our reality and we cannot experience the peace that we deserve as divine beings.

There now exist many techniques and books that help us to understand guilt. There are no excuses to stay in this feeling and to live a mediocre life.

I love how Dr. Hawkins makes us reflect with this question:

> *What is the truth about this journey? The truth is that as we advance inward and discard one illusion after another, one lie after another, one negative program after another, we become lighter and lighter. The*

> *awareness of the presence of love becomes stronger and stronger. We feel lighter and lighter. Life is lived without as much force. Every great teacher since the beginning of time has said that we must look inward and find the truth, because the truth of what is real is what will make us free.*

I had to go through this process with my inner child, which has taken hours upon hours over a course of many years, of reprogramming and reaffirming to myself that nothing that happened had anything to do with me and that it was not my fault. Now my inner child knows perfectly well that she was always innocent. This feeling, as an adult, has left me with a newfound clarity to operate my life in the way that I truly intend and therefore has given me a lot more inner peace.

Now is the moment when you need to take your inner child in your arms and help them to let go of all of that guilt and shame that has accumulated and that you have carried with you over time. Let that child know that they can rest now. Teach them and reprogram them until they accept that nothing that happened was their fault and restore their lost innocence with the unconditional love that you will give them each and every day.

CHAPTER 7

Your Inner Child and Money

> *Would you like to earn more money but are scared because you do not believe that you deserve it? Do you fail to persevere in your efforts, or sabotage them?*

Is there NEVER enough money?

Are you in debt?

Does everything that you start fail?

Do people steal from or defraud you?

Do you have money but still feel rejected or ignore its power?

Do you decide to spend money on things to fill a void that you feel when you are nervous or feel alone?

All of these characteristics are clear examples that you need to heal your inner child. It is worth mentioning that it does not matter if your family had money or not. The relationship that you have with this beautiful energy is either cursed or blessed by the way that your parents handled their properties, businesses, and money in general.

We cannot blind ourselves and think that our inner child does not have anything to do with how we manage our money in the present. It may be that the relationship you have with money is one of love-hate, contempt, cursed, or simply ignored.

My relationship with money was one of "there is no money." It did not matter how much I saw my parents work, their frustration and fights about money were very evident. From a very young age, I learned that there were rich and poor, and that we were poor. I was able to see this difference as early as kindergarten since the school that I went to was one of the nicest in our city. We were able to attend only because they accepted underprivileged kids.

In this school was where I was exposed to the world where my classmates would talk about what Santa Claus would bring them, while he would bring me nothing. Children do not understand finances. They simply feel that something must be wrong with them if they do not receive things while other children do. This was truly a world that I neither belonged to nor understood.

The interesting thing was that in the market, my mother would sell food and drinks, and the money was kept in something that ladies would wear around their waist, like an apron. I would wear one, and while we would sell things, I would collect the money. At the end of the shift, we would count the money, and I would see how much money we would take out of our aprons, only to hear my mother say, "Today was a bad day. We do not have the money necessary for this and that." Without knowing it, my mother was using the law of cause and effect, creating the notion that the money was never enough.

These phrases were saved in my mind, and when I got older, even though my husband was making good money, my mind was programmed to say, "There's not enough, this will not be enough for anything." It took me years to let go of that programming, and it prevented me from experiencing and having truly beautiful things, all because I did not understand what I had accepted in my childhood.

Another thing that programmed me in a very deep and painful way happened as a result of what my father went through when he was tortured. He began to show symptoms of schizophrenia, and one of the symptoms of this is the inability to manage money. My father was always borrowing money from places or people that had high interest rates. A lot of the time, my mother would have to be the one to pay off his debts. It was painful to see the way that he would do what he needed to do, like selling lottery tickets in the street or buying and selling beans. When he was unable to do that anymore, he came to help my mom in the market, making food with her. This is where I saw many fights between them.

In my practice of being a personal coach, I have found interesting the dynamic relationship that people have with money. It does not matter if you were poor or rich while growing up.

In continuation, I will share a few stories from my clients. The names of those involved have been changed for their privacy. The results that they experienced are a direct result of the dedication they have shown in reconnecting and healing their inner children.

Loren was a very successful lady of sixty years, who had various well-established prosperous businesses, living a life of which many would say, "Look at how lucky she is." She came to see me because, although she could take all of the vacations that she wanted, she would feel terribly guilty about it and would instead send her children on beautiful all-inclusive vacations to Rome and Paris. However, she could not seem to treat herself to such luxuries, and she did not really have a reason.

During our inner child session, she recounted a memory of her father who she loved and admired. He owned a successful business and was very respected in their town. In this memory, he had bought a television for his business and one for their home, which was a luxury that many people in their town could not afford. What she noticed in that regression was that her father was always coming home carrying things to eat and always bringing the best tasting food to the house. Afterwards, he would repeat and complain, "Oh how I work and don't have time to rest, and there is never an opportunity to take a vacation."

Loren, the little girl, really enjoyed the things that her father would bring for them. Then she would always hear her father repeat his complaints all the time. When she grew up, she became as successful and even more than her father, but that little girl within held onto the programming that "there is no time to take a vacation because I have to work and work." She managed to talk with her inner child and explain that her father did not understand that he could take a vacation, he simply chose not to and to complain about it instead. With her limited understanding, she accepted the same idea, but now she was going to show her inner child that she had the freedom to enjoy what she had accomplished with her intelligence. It was a process that took her some time, being constant in reprogramming her subconsciousness. And finally, she was able to experience the vacations that she deserved without the guilt and knowing that everything was going to be okay upon her return.

Even in the matters which we think have no explanation, if we give our inner child permission to speak, we see that the lives that we are living are something borrowed. Most of the time, it has nothing to do with you, it is simply a reflection of the programming that you picked up from listening to your parents. These, however, are rarely their own ideas and came from their own parents, and they never realized it.

Camila is a young entrepreneur and full of life. After she was done with school, she started her own business and invested money into her career. The reason she came to see me was that it did not matter which techniques she used, she could not seem to attract clients. She was having little success and was unable to fulfill her dream of buying herself a new car. After going back to her childhood, it was evident that her father, who was a very rich man and belonged to the nicest club in the city, was a despot. She grew up with a lot of fear towards her environment, and even though there was abundance, her inner child accepted that it was better to not have money, because it would cause her to become a despot like her father.

We spoke with her inner child and helped her to see that her father had suffered a lot when he was a child because he had been raised without money, and because of that, he had created a false image of himself, and he had grown into a man without a conscience. She was able to see that this had nothing to do with her nor money. This forgotten paradigm, without her knowing, was blocking her career in the present.

After a few months, she came back to see me and told me with pride that her clientele had increased by 80% and that she had received her first $10,000 payment.

Maritza, a very dedicated, smart lady with great intelligence had opened a jewelry store on one of the main streets in her town. She ran it for many years, and it was very successful, but she ended up losing everything due to the amount of thefts that the store suffered. Her only option was to close down the whole shop. Being an adult, she felt very lost, because she did not know what else to do in order to move ahead, and she did not want to be a burden on her children. What was interesting was that this same thing had happened to her with other businesses, and she did not understand how it could be happening again.

When she came to see me, I could see the pain and her lack of faith, but she gave herself permission to reconnect with her inner child. Going back to her childhood, she was able to remember how her father, an industrious man, would invest in and create businesses only to lose them. The reasons were always different, whether it was due to theft or because the business was not successful. Interestingly, she had noticed that around the same age that she was presently, her father had experienced the worst of luck when thieves left his business with nothing. Finally, he was so disillusioned with life, that he did not want to continue. He developed amnesia and allowed himself to die.

When she had come to see me, her father had passed away ten years prior, meaning that all of this had been forgotten. In the following sessions, she realized that she was repeating the same cycle as her father and that if she did not speak with her inner child, what was waiting for her was to develop an illness and die.

It was beautiful to speak with her inner child and explain to her that now she could create her own life and she did not have to live the same life her father did. That now she was able to use all of that intelligence and create a life that she desired. Maritza knew that it was going to be a process, but she was confident that she would be successful. She felt a lot of gratitude because her father's presence was felt, as if he was giving her his blessing to move forward and to live her own life.

Roberto was a man who had had a lot of money, trips, houses, and cars when he was in his twenties. However, because of a bad investment, he nearly lost everything, including his residence. When he came to my consultation, he was very stressed, full of fear, and with a lot of anger, he would attempt to cover all of these feeling up with a positive attitude.

His question was: Why did he always feel as if he got what he wanted, then something would happen, or a potential investor would back out, and it would be lost? Why would a client who showed so much interest in his product end up going with his competitor or not finalize a deal with him at the last moment?

When he connected with his past, he explained how his mother had left him with an aunt when he was six years old so that she could come to the United States in order to provide for him and promised that she would send for him when she could. Her promise to him wasn't fulfilled until he was twelve years old. He also remembered uncles with lots of kids who also lived in the same house.

These uncles would criticize everything that he did, and he could see that since his mother was gone, the ones who would receive food or gifts or kind words first were his cousins. He was always last. He recounted that from six to ten years old, he had been whipped by his uncles, attempting to correct his wrongdoings, and this made him very sad because he began to believe that he did not deserve anything. His self-esteem dropped, and he became a child with two faces. At school he was happy and popular, but at home, he was very sad and negative.

Speaking with his inner child, he was able to tell him that those people who do not buy from him, did not approve of him, or took their business elsewhere were not his cousins or uncles. That now he would raise him anew, telling him the things that he deserved to hear and treating him how he deserved to be treated.

While working to reconnect with his inner child, he was contracted by a large company and has been able to train his inner child to see life in a more positive way, causing his finances to improve and his anger to disappear.

It needs to be clear that the concept of creating or having a lot of money and living a life of abundance are two very different things. To have money, not share it but only save, is to live with an emptiness that cannot be filled. If you manage to make a million dollars, then you will want two million. However, if on top of having money you live a life of abundance, helping others in need, creating schools and programs that benefit the environment, your community, and your city, your life will increase and be filled. Your inner child can help you with your creativity.

CHAPTER 8

Your Inner Child and Your Relationships

> *"From our partners in life, we ask for the love, attention, and affection that our parents could not give to us. This is unfair to the person who chooses to live with you. Love your inner child and allow them to understand and see that your partner is not your mother or father."* —Mercedes Guzman
>
> *"Oftentimes, the conflicts which are produced in an intimate relationship can be so big that it results in the end of the relationship. However, it is possible that your partner is not responsible for your suffering, they are only someone who reflects a pain that you have carried around for years, as if they were a mirror.* —Paloma Corredor

"But Mercedes," said one of my clients, "what does my inner child have to do with the type of women I am attracting into my life?"

My response was, "Everything, everything René."

This was the start of his process of returning to self-love, to attract the partner that he wanted not the one that his wounded inner child chose.

Who taught you the significance of love? Who showed you to look at love like a synonym of pain? Have you wondered why you have the concepts of men and women? How many times were your parents arguing and during that time abandoned you and your siblings emotionally, and now that fear rises to the surface and leaves you unable to trust anyone?

Or maybe your mom or dad abandoned home, or died, and you were left young and helpless, creating this emptiness in your heart, and no one explained to you why it happened. Perhaps you took onto your own shoulders the responsibility of keeping the relationship between your parents working, and in the end, you were unable to do it when they sat you down to tell you that they were getting a divorce. Could it be that you father may have physically abused your mother in front of you, and because you were little, you could not do anything about it? Or maybe it was the other way around, and your mother was abusing your father. Did you see your mother crying because you father did not come home, and you later found out that he was cheating on her? Or that your mother cheated on your father?

Now in the present, do you wish to get married but attract partners into your life who do not value you or who do not fill what you were looking for? It is time that you connect with your inner child and heal your relationships so that your children and their children can live in harmony and love their partners as well as their children.

I knew that Father loved my mother, but I saw that Mother could not fully express the love that she had for him because she resented him. This was evident as she would always show by yelling, demanding, and pushing my father away while creating a mechanism for sickness, albeit unconsciously. In my little-girl eyes, it was a love-hate relationship. Now I can see the cause of it, but when I was little, I learned to always be on my mother's side and to begin to see all of the faults that my father had. I learned that men were the source of all our issues, that they do not provide like they should, that they are cheaters, they make you suffer, and then they can also abandon you. My mother was very controlling due to the way in which she was raised, and she would not let us do much. We would have to ask her permission for everything.

I grew up, and I had three significant relationships. The first one lasted two years, and I got tired of it and ended it. In the second one, the man left me after four years of us dating on and off and got married to someone else. This really hurt me, but I released the pain, and a year later I met my husband. When we got married, without knowing it, I put my husband in the "mother" category and began, without being conscious of it, my training to be a victim. I would ask his permission for everything. A lot of the times, he would be in meetings, and I would call him and call him until he would finally answer, then I would ask things like, "Can I have permission to take the children to McDonald's?" Sometimes he would say no, and from a place that I did not understand, I would feel this strong pain and resentment towards him. This was aggravating our situation.

I would complain about how he would treat me and how I could not believe that he was that way. But I could not speak with anyone about him, and so I would just swallow all my pain. It did not take away the fact that he would act in a way that was very harsh with me and would treat me in very hurtful ways sometimes, but now I understand that, no one can make you feel any way, unless you give them the permission to. But my inner child did not know that, since I did not even have any idea that it was her governing my relationship with my husband specifically during that time of pain.

Time went on, I had my fifth child, and it was there that I realized that I no longer loved my husband. But I could not leave him or get a divorce because I did not work at the time and I had five little ones to take care of.

I found myself in what many teachers call "the dark night of the soul." I had no joy, and I felt trapped. I would just throw all of my anger and blame onto my husband. In order to justify how I felt, I would blame him for my pain, for our lack of money, for giving our sons a bad example of how to treat a woman. It was a time of a deep sense of self-pity, but it caused my search to deepen. I began to say and affirm which I still teach today, and that is, "God, let me see my husband through the eyes of love."

Just as this beautiful power always listens, my husband's older sister called me one day and recounted to me what he went through as a child. She told me how his mother died when he was only three years old, and because his father had to work, he would be left with people who would treat him terribly, and they were constantly having to move from house to house. This happened between the ages of three to nine years old. It was during this time that he would receive all kinds of rejections and teasing. Then his father died in an accident, and no one wanted to be left in charge of him. Finally, one of their aunts agreed to take him in, but that is another whole story of abandonment and pain in his life. I knew none of this, as he would never speak about it. This caused a birth of compassion towards him.

I prayed for celestial guidance in order to fall in love with my husband again, and in the process, a very clear message was given to me: "He is the only man with whom you will reach enlightenment in this life. He is the only one." This is where my restoration began, and I talked to my inner child, and I showed her that my husband was not Mother. It has been a long process, but now I can say that the one who is with my husband is now the adult. My inner child knows her place. My deepest wish was to have a spiritual relationship, and now it is, and I know that it will only get better because there are many levels of self-love and self-discovery.

Natalia and Alberto had been together for many years. At the beginning of their relationship, everything had been going well. When they came to see me, I could feel that they loved each other, but it seemed as if Alberto did not really care about the relationship and appeared as if he would rather hang out with his friends. I began working with them, but at one point, Alberto decided not to return. Natalia kept coming back for her sessions. The moment came when she found out that Alberto had been unfaithful. It was a very difficult time, but they had to separate.

Alberto quickly realized the big mistake he had made, and he came back to see me on his own to heal his inner child. This took some time, and after a while, Natalia restarted her sessions as well. Alberto was a young man who had suffered a very traumatic childhood. His father abandoned his family, and his mother began going out with lots of different men. He was exposed to this life, and there was really nothing that he could do. He grew up with resentment and a lack of affection. He was a very athletic young man, who was very attractive, and although he would attract many women, his life felt empty. When he met Natalia, he felt a celestial confirmation that she was the woman that he would be with for the rest of his life. She did not know who he was, but eventually they found each other and began their lives together.

Natalia came from a marriage in which her father was unfaithful and did not value her mother. When she was thirteen years old, they got a divorce, and she switched between living a week with her father, and then a week with her mother, and this gave her a sense of instability.

Infidelity is a wound that can heal, but it leaves a very big scar on a relationship. The people in the relationship must learn to live with the doubt, but this will not necessarily destroy the relationship. Alberto and Natalia managed to heal their inner children. They ended up getting married and have been living a very pleasant life, now that they are adults living together and not two children who are looking for their parents.

Carolina was a young lady who was very quick to smile and could not stop laughing nervously, even when she was talking about things that were very simple. She came to see me because the relationship with her spouse was one of a lot of verbal abuse, which oftentimes led to physical abuse as well. She was tired and did not understand what was causing this. Even though she knew logically that she had to leave him, something in her mind was not allowing her to act.

In our conversation, she told me that her education was cut short when her father abandoned their family, and she was forced to begin working in order to help out with the costs of the house when she was only ten years old. Her mother, an uneducated lady, had been leaving them at their grandmother's house from the time that they were very young so that she could go and work, because her father was an alcoholic and did not seem to be there for them. Her grandmother was very cruel and would incessantly beat her grandchildren.

Because Carolina was the oldest, she would receive the majority of the beatings from her grandmother, and then from her own mother as well, as the grandmother would constantly complain about Carolina to the mother. In her session with me, she was able to realize how she would receive the beating from her grandmother for no apparent reason. She remembered how one day, when she was eight years old, her grandmother had come to where she was and had yelled at her, humiliated her, and then beat her in front of the neighbors. In order to dissimulate with the pain and the shame that she felt in that moment, she developed a nervous laugh, which began to arise each time that she would be punished or humiliated. She was using this as a defense mechanism, in order to calm her anxiety of what was happening. This was the reason why as an adult she would laugh all the time, but mostly when she was nervous.

Additionally, she was also able to see how her mother would make it very clear that she was punishing her because she cared about her and wanted to make sure that she did not grow up to be a nobody, just another street person. Along with this, she would reinforce to her that it was better to be with just one man then to have various lovers. This was the repetitive story that her mom would tell her all the time as she was punishing her when Carolina had not washed the dishes or had not helped out with something around the house.

Carolina grew up with that programming, and when she wanted to leave her relationship, which was obviously damaging, all of these phrases from her mother would be repeating unconsciously and would not allow her to leave or report him once and for all. Her thought process was that he was doing it because he loved her. After various sessions, she managed to speak with her inner child, forgive her mother and grandmother, reclaim her power as a woman, and not allow herself to be the victim anymore. Her process began, and finally she was able to leave her abusive relationship. Luckily the union had not created children yet. She moved to a new town and was able to get a better job. She is in a much healthier relationship today.

Silvia a very pretty young woman, an executive, and a divorcée with a lot of amazing qualities. She is intelligent, educated, and sweet. However, in relationship experiences, everything turned out very traumatic. She came to see me, and during our conversation she commented that in the relationships she had been in, her partners would not value her. They were liars, and there was always a lot of resentment and anger. One thing of note was that she would always attract men who made less money than she did. In her heart, she knew that she wanted someone who was going to treat her like a princess because that was what she deserved.

When we went back to her childhood, we were able to see that her parents were always fighting and arguing in front of her. Because of her character, she took it upon herself to make peace between them. Her father, who was a very strong businessman, would treat her mother in a very degrading way. As for Silvia, he never valued her, even though she was the only child. He would never go to her school nor accompanied her to anything. She would do everything to try to please her father, but he never made her feel like she deserved the best.

Her mother, on the other hand, would play the role of the victim but had a very passive aggressive attitude. Without knowing it, Salvia's inner child made a promise that she would never marry someone like her father, who would put down her mother for not having a job. When she grew up, she forgot about this, but it was still saved in her subconsciousness. There was the reason why she would attract men who were making less than she was. This was so that they would not look down on her. The rage and resentment that she held towards her father would cause her, at the slightest feeling of being lied to or disrespected, to explode easily and start her pain. Her partners would get tired and would not see the grand woman that she was, because she would unknowingly hide under a mask that was very hard, when in reality she was feeling very lonely with a lot of fear on the inside. When we freed her inner child, and she was able to understand all of her programming, immediately she was able to attract into her life a very handsome man who was an engineer and who now treats her like a complete princess.

CHAPTER 9

Your Inner Child and Sexual Orientation

> *"A boy of five years old does not know what sex is, but even at that young age, he can be aware that instead of liking girls, he feels something very nice that he cannot explain when he looks at boys. The feeling is the same with little girls."* —Mercedes Guzman

This is a topic that in the last few years has become more accepted, although in the past it has been look at as taboo. For that reason, I chose to add a chapter in this book pertaining to this subject. Diverse sexual orientation has been condemned even to this day by religion and governments of many countries. Thousands have died by the hands of people who are homophobic. This condemnation is rejection, fear, prejudice, and discrimination against the men and women who know themselves as homosexual.

Recently on Facebook, the photographer Brandon Stanton, creator of *Humans of New*

York, photographed a young boy of ten years old who had a lot of emotional anguish, in which the boy was quoted saying, "I am homosexual, and my future scares me because it will displease people." He is not alone in that feeling, as thousands of homosexuals wish not to be. Many of them hate themselves for feeling what they feel.

I have had the blessing of meeting many inner children through my gay clients. In speaking with them, it gives me such tenderness and pain to see how at such a young age, they knew what they felt, but knowing they would immediately feel rejected by their parents, teachers, religion, and friends is something very strongly felt. As intelligent kids, many managed to evade the feeling and try to camouflage themselves by becoming like everyone else. Involving themselves in sports, creating a masculine body, and having girlfriends. The girls cover up their reality by becoming overly obedient to their mothers, who may suspect something but are in denial of it, all in an attempt to protect them, not wanting to accept reality. Some youths may even become homophobic themselves in an effort to hide who they are.

I want to be clear that many of these kids have not been sexually abused, and the boys that have been abused by men or the girls that have been abused by women oftentimes are heterosexual, showing that sexual abuse is not the cause of a child being gay. In my experience, I have learned the children who are homosexual are not changed to be that way, they are born like that.

I personally was abused sexually by a woman, yet I remember very clearly when I was five years old liking a boy in kindergarten. I even remember his name to this date. Tito would take me by the hand during recess and walk me over to the collection of snakes that some teachers used to show their class. I remember how my little heart would begin to beat very quickly, and I did not understand why. This same feeling happens to children who are gay, when at that point, they know nothing about sexuality.

The sexual abuse that many heterosexual children experience leaves a lot of confusion, and many times as adults they may have sexual fantasies with people of their same sex, which leads to feelings of guilt and shame.

Many of them experience sexual relations with members of the same sex, but they will always feel as if something is not right.

You can successfully dissipate this sexual confusion and pain to become an adult who is sexually centered and healthy by connecting with your inner child, being conscious and confronting any abuses, and finding a professional in that field to help and support you to be able to enjoy this necessary part of life.

National Geographic magazine published the following:

> *The brains of gay people share characteristics with those of heterosexual people from the opposite sex, a new study shows. Investigators have found similarities in the physical structure and size of the brain as well as in the strength of the neurological connections between gay people and heterosexuals of the opposite sex.*
>
> *In some respects, the brains of heterosexual males and lesbians are similar in respect to the length of brain waves, as studies*

> *show. In the same manner, gay males and heterosexual females have the same brain similarities. This finding shows evidence that homosexuals may have a genetic predisposition which causes them to be gay. The differences in the brain activity and the anatomy were observed in a study that included ninety men and women including homosexuals and heterosexuals of both sexes. The investigators observed the neural brain activity by measuring the blood flow. The results of these explorations show that both sides of the brain also change in their symmetry depending on the sexual orientation of the person.*

José, an intelligent young man who had graduated with honors from a university, was using drugs and alcohol and could not maintain a stable job. He had been dating his girlfriend for a few months. She was very lovely, and they loved each other. He was very popular and well liked amongst his friends due to the nature of his character. In our meeting, he told me that during his childhood, he was the victim of a lot of bullying and that even in his current jobs, he was the target of bullying from his superiors.

When he came to me, he was tired and without hope. The cycles of pain and lack of self-acceptance had returned, causing him feelings of depression. One of his dreams was to move to a big city and work in art, which was his passion. But because of everything that was happening, this dream seemed like a distant reality.

When we went back to his childhood, José realized that ever since he was six years old, he began feeling attracted to boys, but his spontaneity as a child that showed these feelings caused a lot of insecurity in his teachers. This was where his persecutions began. In his childhood, he suffered depression and was prescribed medication, which would work for a time, but once again the pain would come back. His father would support him, but José was never able to tell his parents that he was gay.

In connecting with his inner child, he was able to carefully observe what had gone on during that time and to tell his inner child that he was a normal child. That it was okay what he felt and that it was not his fault. He was able to admit what he had denied for many years and was able to say, "I am gay, Mercedes. I am gay." There was a peace that shined in his eyes as a smile painted his face, and he made the decision that he would first tell his girlfriend then his family. And that was how he came to be himself.

Within three weeks, he was able to move to the desired city, and he is now living without shame or guilt and without having to hide his true identity.

Relationships in gay couples

The issues that gay couples have are not different from the issues that exist in heterosexual relationships. In my practice, I have had many cases involving couples, and when I am in front of a gay couple, I see that the issues are the same.

It is the lack of acceptance, not valuing each other, of not loving each other, that produces discord in relationships. When a gay person works with their inner child, they are able to accept, love, and value themselves. This can then be seen reflected in their life and relationships. (See Chapter 8: Your Inner Child and Your Relationships.)

CHAPTER 10

Your Inner Child and Health

> *"A resentment, largely cultivated, can deteriorate the body until it converts itself into the illness that we call cancer."*
> —Louise Hay

It is incredible to think that our illnesses in the present have a lot to do with what was programed in what we lived with as children. Many of my clients when they come to see me do not mention their illnesses. Instead, they simply tell me about their relationships, but it is very clear to see, as many great scientists and spiritual teachers have said, "Everything is connected to everything. You cannot separate a part from the whole." Once you heal your mind, your sickness will disappear.

If you take a close look back into your past, you will see how many times illnesses were used to manipulate partners, whether it was your mother or your father using it. Another phenomenon that you may see is that sickness may have been the only way that your mother would receive love and attention from your father, so you learned that your sickness could bring the same attention.

I have a client who was hospitalized many times when she was a child, and it was only in the hospital where she would find peace and smiling people who cared for her. Now in the present, even though she understands the power of thoughts her inner child created, her body manifested a sickness in which she was required to visit the hospital every few months to be observed. We had a session and talked with her inner child, and it is going to be interesting how her doctor will eventually tell her that she is healed and does not have to return.

> *"Let us clarify that it is the wish or will of the adult whether they want to continue to be controlled by their inner child or if they really want to become an adult. —Mercedes Guzman*

Negative energy from the constant injustice of one of your parents, stress lived at home, resentment for being humiliated, abandonment, the beatings, and even the absence of your caretakers is being stored in your emotional body and subconscious. Then as you grow older, these wounds open, and your reality becomes opaque by the perception of your pain and eventually comes out as disease and illnesses, such as rheumatism, high blood pressure, cancer, or high cholesterol, to keep creating the same cycle of pain that was never dealt with as a child.

> *"A man is not defiled by what enters his mouth but by what comes out of it."*
> —*Matthew 15:11*

It is of total importance that you reconnect and reprogram your inner child and let go of all those stored thoughts and feelings. Science together with medicine has done countless studies that show how the effects of our thoughts, beliefs, and feelings create, almost instantly and miraculously, disease or remission thereof. The surprising conclusion of these studies is that when someone is healed of their illness through a placebo, it is because nurses, doctors, and hospital staff put in the extra effort that made the affected person feel attended to, that they mattered, and that they were important. That goes to say that their inner child received what they were longing for and the adult had forgotten.

> *"And so, to my lovely nurses and doctors, when you see a patient who keeps returning to the emergency room, use your imagination and mentally pretend that you are speaking with their inner child. Tell them that they deserve to be healed. Tell them to love and value themselves so that they do not have to keep returning. Or refer them to a psychologist who deals with the inner child in order to help them heal their emotional wounds."*
> —Mercedes Guzman

The desire of all human beings is to be loved and valued. However, many of these adults do not realize that what a child needed while growing was not provided. In their place were forgotten children, mistreated, and their emotional needs were negated.

CHAPTER 11

Parents Can Create Illnesses in Their Children

There is a syndrome known as Munchausen syndrome. In 1951, Dr. Richard Asher, a British endocrinologist and hematologist defined this mental aliment, which is also known by its variant, factitious disorder. With this syndrome, an adult produces or fakes illness in a child under their care, generally sons or daughters but also nieces and nephews or even unrelated children being cared for by a nanny who suffers from the effects of this syndrome.

Many mothers are affected by this syndrome without knowing it, and its effects can be very devastating because the power of the subconscious mind only obeys but does not question and is directed to create what we constantly assert in our minds. This is where a parent or caretaker essentially does the same thing but instead projects the supposed illness onto the child in their care.

There exists a large percentage of mothers, who unconsciously with their thoughts and their feelings, create the illness in their own children. The majority of these mothers have lived lives that were very difficult and traumatic in their childhood. During the time of choosing a life partner, they attract relationships that put them in similar circumstances such as pain, abandonment, rejection, and humiliation. In the midst of their relationship problems, they may become pregnant and unconsciously do not understand that what they are feeling at such a deep level is actually affecting the fetus that is developing, that is already feeling and receiving all the mother is experiencing. I have had clients who in their pregnancy lived fearfully and worried about their child being born sick. Mothers not knowing of the power of their thoughts and feelings do not look for a way to change that way of thinking but continue with their pain, feeling as if they are victims of circumstance, thus creating stress in the formation of the fetus. (I would like to clear up that I am not attempting to cover up the dad's error. This is another subject, see Chapter 8: You Inner Child and Your Relationships.)

The mothers would not want to harm their babies in any way, but without begin aware, their own inner children, who did not know better, continue accepting and observing that the only way to feel love for your parents was to worry about them or that only during sickness would their parents unite and demonstrate love. Your inner child has to protect you and goes to look for similar solutions, and one of these is to create the disease to see if at least the pain, abandonment, and rejection that the adult mother is feeling presently may disappear. Recreating this pattern once again and without knowing it is giving life to a sad reality that affects their babies. These recreated illnesses in their children can range from autism, lung disease, viruses, cancer, and even death.

CHAPTER 12

Your Inner Child and Sickness

> *"The bio-cognitive perspective offers a unified model in which the cultural beliefs, as well as spiritual, influences the biological processes which affect your health."*
> —Dr. Mario E. Martinez

Ever since I was old enough to use reason, I would always see my mother suffer with illness. I remember the intense feeling of being powerless against her pain, and I would see her many times in bed or sometimes even in the hospital. It was as if every time she would create a new illness, and there would be an energy of blame, as I perceived it, as if I were responsible for what happened to Mom, and therefore the pressure was to be more obedient. Because we did not have medical insurance and the pharmacies in my country were not regulated, many people would self-medicate. However, medicine was not cheap, and it was for this reason that we would use herbs as often as we could. We would hear phrases like, "Don't walk around barefoot or you will catch a cold," and "If you don't eat, you will get sick." I grew up with cana fistula for parasites, Vicks VapoRub or menthol, lime, and honey for coughs and colds, Alka-Seltzer for stomach pain, and aspirin for any other sort of pain.

I remember that in my mind, I accepted that sickness would come, and you had no control over it. When I reached the age where I began to get my period, I would be in a lot of pain, but my mother would get very worried, and it was in these times that I felt like she really cared about me. What was interesting was that the pain would always come during the night, and I would spend hours dealing with that pain. My mother would always wake up and help me through it. It was as if my mind would say, "Now I get to spend time with my mother, all by myself." At least that is how I see it now.

When I turned twelve years old, my father's mother, Grandma Maria, got dementia. She began to act like a little girl, would call out for her own mother, and was not be able to sleep at night. They brought her to live with us, and I remember that I would calm her down because she thought that I was her mother. I loved my grandmother a lot. She passed away when I was fifteen. A few years after that, the same illness began to affect my father. I had unconsciously accepted that I would be next. My mother, in her ignorance and because she did not understand my character, would always tell me that I was too nervous. Because of that programming, I began to develop nervous ticks in my face, constipation, and throat problems. Issues that I now know are produced by the conditioning during the time I was raised.

At twenty years old, I stayed away from doctors, and if I felt any sort of ailment, I would look for cures in the way that I knew. When I got married at the age of twenty-three, I got pregnant twice, and my body aborted the fetuses. This was a very sad and painful experience that led me to visit doctors and to take pills that were very strong. My husband was raised in the same way when it came to medicine. They did not have the money to get checkups or have a family doctor. He did not even like taking pain pills such as aspirin or Tylenol.

When I was twenty-six, I got pregnant again. We moved from El Salvador to Texas. This was where my first daughter, Yanica, was born in a hospital. Since I was Mormon, and it was my duty, within a year I was pregnant again. My husband was just starting his own construction company, and we did not have medical insurance, so with the prompting of church members who had done it, we decided to have our second child at home.

During the process of awakening to my inner child, I began to read a very powerful book that helped to reinforce the knowledge that we create with our thoughts. The book is *Basic Principles of the Science of Mind* by Dr. Frederick Bailes. Since I birthed my next four children at home, I worked with midwifes and naturopathic doctors. Until that point, I had only used herbs to heal my children. We had not been taking them to pediatricians. With that book, I learned the power of "scientific prayer," which is the process of deep feeling and giving thanks for that which you have asked for. I began to apply this concept in my life because I felt exhausted, having had five children in the span of six and a half years and choosing to homeschool them. There would be nights that for different reasons, one or more of my children would wake me up. I had also chosen to breastfeed my baby, and there were many nights I would not sleep at all, which only added to my exhaustion.

In my desperation, I began to use the concept of scientific prayer. When one of my children began to cough, sniffle, or moan, I would immediately begin to repeat a scientific prayer. It would go like this: I would say the name of my child, then repeat the following, "Is a child of the light, who is healed and perfect. Their lungs are healthy. They rest and will wake up feeling happy. I turn this over to God, knowing that this is already given." Miraculously, this worked most of the time, and I felt such a sense of gratitude because I would not have to even get up. I began to develop a lot of faith in this process, which even reduced my use of herbs to focus more on prayer.

Because I was also homeschooling then, I would include this teaching daily, and they learned to accept that they could be healed if their own mind accepted it. To this day, if one of them gets a cold or is not feeling well, instead of running to a doctor, they take the healing upon themselves using herbs and vitamins to support the natural healing process.

Personally, I stopped counting the more than twenty years I have not visited doctors. Every time I feel something off in my body, I turn once again to the scientific prayer, and it has worked every time. I invite you to educate yourself on how to heal your own body with alternative medicine and meditation. Take some time to study "great minds" who use and teach these processes.

CHAPTER 13

Success and Your Inner Child

> *"Just like an inexhaustible well brings forth water, in that same way, your forgotten inner child can bring forth infinite amounts of success in your life."* —Mercedes Guzman

Ever since I began to awaken back in 1997, I embarked on a quest to find the knowledge and understanding of how the mind and emotions work and how these are governed by our brain. I set the intention to learn and apply all that was necessary in order to calm the pain that I felt. Through prayer, I asked God to allow me to reach levels of knowledge that I did not even know existed. I began to read the few books that I had and noticed that the universe would send me information through many other books, which would come to me in miraculous ways, and my time was consumed by reading for interminable hours.

Without knowing the process I was going through, I began to notice many people at the church that we attended at the time would seek me out for advice. My heart opened up, and I felt this grand calling to help those around me.

There was a divine force that was guiding me. I was being divinely trained on how to more consciously work with my emotions. I started feeling how this power would give me homework to see if I had learned the concepts of forgiveness, acceptance, etc. Then would come the exams on all subjects of life. Everything that I was learning would be tested. I felt as if I graduated with a doctorate degree from life through an emotional, physical, and spiritual process, which lasted many years. Then the time came to go out into the field and show others how to do the same.

The lives of many have been transformed by my counseling. They then started referring me to others, and that is how my name became as a chain. After seven years of learning, one-on-one coaching, and preparedness, I made the decision in 2004 to take my teaching to the next level. I took a class on public speaking. I then applied my learnings by giving classes on metaphysics at a spiritual center named Unity North. The church had a goal, and a Hispanic group was formed. The group attendance was increasing every Thursday. I began to notice the emergence of fears, doubts, low self-esteem. *Am I doing this right? What if this is not what I am supposed to do?* While the questions were plaguing my mind, there was no turning back. God had a higher purpose for me.

Because of the discussions that I would have with my husband, many times I was tempted to stop giving these classes and stay at home and be a wife, mother, and housekeeper. We were investing our money to give these free classes because charging for them gave me so much shame. In my mind and pain, I thought my husband resisted the idea of me being a public figure. Without knowing it at the time, this was a period of learning, which would show me all of my programming about money and success I had accepted as a child. I now know my inner child was sabotaging my dreams. Success is personal, and if what you are doing is not producing any economic results, your loved ones will not understand. Success is a process that takes time, but if you show your inner child that they deserve success, it will happen faster.

> *"Success is going from failure to failure without losing your enthusiasm."* —Winston Churchill

During 2005, having no money in the bank due to our lack of knowledge on how to manage our finances and our programming in relation to money, maintaining faith and vision, we applied the law of attraction to miraculously purchase and move into a beautiful new house with new furniture in a beautiful area. During this time, my husband also got a new job that paid a six-figure income. It was as if the universe orchestrated everything in such a beautiful way so that our desires were being manifested step by step.

This change in our lives gave me the confidence and authority to continue to teach, as I was able to show by example what can happen when you apply these principles. If my life was able to transform into a picture of wealth and abundance through the processes that I was talking about, then I knew that it would work for others as well. This was reinforced, as the group that I was teaching would grow each and every week.

Even with all these manifestations and abundance, I was still suffering in relation to money. I felt as if I did not deserve it, but this was something that I kept in silence. During that time, I did not pay much attention to my forgotten inner child, and she would scream her fears about money, but unconsciously I would not listen to her. However, in my moments of desperation, I asked for guidance, and there were times I would throw myself on the floor, crying out, "I cannot do this anymore, this is too painful. How can I possibly speak of abundance when I feel this way?" It seems that each time I asked, I would experience a miracle in my life that would restore my faith and get me back on track.

This was just the beginning of a new cycle. In 2008, we moved to Florida because my husband had been offered an excellent job earning more money. I left the Hispanic group at Unity North, but people were still coming to me for help and advice. Some began asking me if I could speak to their family or friends in other countries and give them sessions. This was when I realized that this was something that I could do around the world using technology. That was how I began counseling and coaching people around the world.

When I got to Florida, I began to study more with the internet. I created a YouTube channel that is viewed around the world to this day. Then through a connection with a friend, I met a lady in El Paso, Texas, who conducted a program on Univision Radio. For two years, the radio show would call me every Thursday, and I would give a message of inspiration. A person from El Paso began to contact me through e-mail, offering to build my website, so I decided to do it. We called the site Talk to Mercedes, the same as my radio segment at the time.

Due to the recession, in 2010, my husband lost his job. Overnight, it seemed as if everything was about to fall apart, but we began applying everything that we had learned. The day that he called me to tell me that he had lost his job, I told him that we should go celebrate at one of the nicest restaurants that we could find, and that was what we did.

That was when I got the idea to give conferences. The universe opened the roads, and I went to El Paso and Mexico to share a message of hope in the middle of the economic crisis. It was a period of much gratitude, as we were able to see that all of the work and effort that I had put into my awakening was paying dividends and expanding. We saw the hand of the divine manifesting even in the smallest of things.

> *"Miracles happen to those who believe in them. In order to be a realist, you must believe in miracles. Seeing, hearing, and feeling are miracles, and each part and tag of me is a miracle. There are two ways to live: you can live as if nothing is a miracle; you can live as if everything is a miracle."*
> *—Albert Einstein*

Since 2009, everything made a big turn, and more miracles began to manifest in my life. A beautiful person that I knew during that time told me that in order to do what I was doing legally, since I was not a psychologist, I should become an ordained revered, and I became a reverend. Since then, I have been giving conferences and workshops of all types in different countries around the world. I have met some very important people who have helped me along my journey. I have gotten the opportunity to advise all different types of people, including diplomats, artists, mothers, children, millionaires, etc. I have received awards and recognitions, have written various articles including a feature in Forbes Magazine. I continue to be interviewed on various channels like CNÑ and radio shows. I am being invited to give conferences to various groups.

It has not been easy. I have had many obstacles and have fallen and gotten back up. I have suffered humiliation, rejection, abandonment, and teasing but have learned that nothing comes to destroy me, everything comes to elevate me. I know that as long as we live, there is no end to our journey. We continue to move forward and bless thousands through our example.

To this day, I still speak to my little Merceditas. She is now closer to me than ever. Her innocence and intelligence give me such tenderness, strength, and confidence to move ahead. I always keep her updated on what is happening, and I invite her to always be with me. She is the medium through which I am connected to God and the divine.

I invite you not to give up on your dreams and to not give up on your forgotten inner child. Connect with them and transform your adult with their help, and the success that is yours by divine right will be at hand.

CHAPTER 14

Practical Exercises to Reconnect With Your Forgotten Child

> *"Imagination is more important than knowledge."* —Albert Einstein

Let your inner child tell you how they feel

Find a comfortable spot where you can write. Take a piece of paper and a pen with you and play some soothing meditative music that will relax your mind. Let your intention be to bring out all of the memories that you remember in your first five years. Do not try to justify any adults, just listen to how your inner child is feeling, even if the adult feels the child deserved what happened to them or if you feel they were misbehaved, dishonest, or lazy. Give that inner child the opportunity to tell you what they really felt at that young age.

Speak with your inner child

Your inner child loves when you call them by name with tenderness. Every time that you feel anguish, pain, anger, frustration, or rage, speak with your inner child in a loving and gentle manner. Say your name to yourself the way you were called as a child. For example, say "Charlie, we are going to let go of this anger, I love you. Thank you," or, "Loren, my little girl, let go of this sadness, okay? Thank you, I love you." This activates your subconscious to listen and understand. Eventually it will begin to allow you to release the stories that are provoking these feelings.

Your inner child will help you with relationship problems

Every night, take a few minutes before you go to sleep to call your inner child by their name. Ask them to show you what they accepted in regard to love and relationships, and then tell them that they do not need to look for Mom or Dad in their partner. If you do not have a partner, tell them to stop looking for Mom or Dad in a partner and that you as an adult will look for the person that you wish to spend your life with.

Your inner child will help you with financial issues

Take a piece of paper and write down, "My child, what do you feel when I say the word *money*?" Then take a moment to breathe deeply and allow your inner child to guide your writing. Together, let go of all the memories of lack, persons, pain, and fear that you have around money. Tell that child that they deserve to have wealth and abundance.

Affirmation: My inner child and I accept infinite abundance. I love money and money loves me. I give it with love and know that it returns to me multiplied.

You can teach your inner child kindness

Every time that you feel and observe emotions such as irritation, resentment, and sadness, do not try to suppress them. Instead, realize that these emotions come from a variety of memories that have been stored since you were a child. Close your eyes, connect with your inner child of ten years old or whichever age the feelings may be coming from. Call them by their name and imagine them standing in front of you. Picture yourself getting down on their level. Look them in the eyes and tell them, "It was not your fault, it never was, and it never will be." Give them a hug and tell them to stay with you. Being friendly with yourself helps you develop a genuine relationship with your inner child. In place of feeling bad for feeling the way that you do, accept them and let them go. Then you will have space to be good to yourself, your inner child, and those around you.

Your inner child needs tender and stimulating words

Speak with your inner child the way that you would have wished that the adults around you spoke when you were that age. For example, say, "It is not your fault that you feel inferior to your cousin," "Do not worry, this will pass soon," "You are incredible," "You are intelligent," "Please forgive me that I spoke to you that way," "You do belong," or "You are enough." If you liked to draw, sing, dance, give yourself the permission to do so and sign up for some classes as an adult and bring your inner child with you to those classes. You will begin to see your life expanding every day.

Involve your inner child in your life daily

Have you noticed how excited kids get when you ask for their help? Our inner children react the same way. Every time that you need additional help, in a very friendly manner, call your inner child and say, "Will you please help me finish this project?" or, "Can you please help me solve this issue that I am having with my partner?" You will begin to notice how quickly your energy will change in regard to the subject. The wisdom, creativity, and inspiration that is inside all of us is held in our inner children, and when we ask for their help, it becomes available to us.

Your inner child needs to develop patience

Impatience is a program in our inner child that causes a lot of issues. It is a sign that as you grew up, there was no space to make errors. That any issues should have been resolved immediately. Allow yourself to make mistakes and know that it is okay. Nothing big was built in a day. Emotional healing also means setting aside anything that is not adding to a positive emotional environment. When you feel impatience, hug yourself while picturing that you are hugging your inner child and make a "shhhshhh" sound for a few moments. Your impatience, anger, and frustration will diminish, and little by little you will see the solution.

Journey back in time with your inner child

This technique can help you immensely! Each night, take a few minutes to observe your day, and try to find anything that bothered you, whether that be an argument you had with your boss, an issue with your own child, or maybe with your spouse, family, or friends. Then call your inner child by their name and notice which age they appear as. Let's say they appeared as an eight-year-old. Use your imagination to take that child by the hand. Breathe deeply three times and travel to that specific point in time in your mind to observe what was really happening while you were that age. Then ask yourself why you are creating the situation that is giving you issues in the present.

Now, with the understanding that you have as an adult, explain to that child what was really happening. For example, in one case where I was arguing with my husband over money, I called my inner child and she appeared as a ten-year-old girl. I asked her why I had gotten so upset with my husband, and in that moment, a memory arose of when I wanted a new pair of shoes and my mother could not buy them for me. In the present, I wanted something, but my husband was telling me that we could not get it because of the money. In that moment, I spoke to my inner child and told her. "Daniel, my husband, is not my mother. If I desired to buy what I wanted, I can do it without asking permission." Very quickly, I felt at peace, and the anger that I felt towards my husband disappeared.

Mentally speak with your inner child, softly release the memory of the past, and visualize a beautiful light filling the new space with love. Then go with your inner child to the beach or someplace where you feel at peace, and imagine that the two of you shout the word FREEDOM three times.

Conclusion

It is my desire that these pages bring you hope, peace, and confidence that there is a road to reach heaven, and your inner child has the power to transport you back to our natural state of love and innocence.

With each day that passes, I feel so thankful to see how my life continues to transform because of my connection with my inner child. I invite you to share this book so that the miracle of returning to love and innocence by reconnecting with our forgotten children continues to manifest in this world.

I end my book with a message that comes to us from *A Course in Miracles*, lesson 182, referring to our inner child:

> *There is a Child in you Who seeks His Father's house and knows that He is a stranger here. Their childhood is eternal with an innocence that will endure forever. Where this Child shall go is holy ground. It is His Holiness that lights up Heaven, and that brings to earth the pure reflection of the*

light above, wherein are earth and Heaven joined as one.

It is this Child in you your Father knows as His Own Son. It is this Child Who knows His Father. He desires to go home so deeply, so unceasingly, His voice cries unto you to let Him rest a while. He does not ask for more than just a few instants of respite; just an interval in which He can return to breathe again the holy air that fills His Father's house. You are His home as well. He will return. But give Him just a little time to be Himself, within the peace that is His home, resting in silence and in peace and love.

This Child needs your protection. He is far from home. He is so little that He seems so easily shut out, His tiny voice so readily obscured, His call for help almost unheard amid the grating sounds and harsh and rasping noises of the world. Yet does He know that in you still abides His sure protection. You will fail Him not. He will go home, and you along with Him.

This Child is your defenselessness; your strength. He trusts in you. He came because

He knew you would not fail. He whispers of His home unceasingly to you. For He would bring you back with Him, that He Himself might stay, and not return again where He does not belong, and where He lives an outcast in a world of alien thoughts. His patience has no limits. He will wait until you hear His gentle Voice within you, calling you to let Him go in peace, along with you, to where He is at home and you with Him.

Bibliography

Books

The Child, the Family, and the Outside World - D. W. Winnicott - Penguin - 1991

The Divine Matrix - Gregg Braden - 2007

Basic Principles of the Science of Mind - Frederik Bailes - June 1, 1951

Homecoming: Reclaiming and Championing Your Inner Child - John Bradshaw - February 1, 1992

The Power of Intention - Dr. Wayne Dyer - August 1, 2005

The Biology of Belief - Bruce H. Lipton, Ph.D. - Hay House - November 30, 2007

You Can Heal Your Life - Louise Hay - Hay House - September 1, 1992

Letting Go: The Pathway of Surrender - Dr. David Hawkins - 2014

The Law of Attraction: The basis of the teachings of Abraham - Esther and Jerry Hicks - November 1, 2007

A Course in Miracles - Foundation for Inner Peace - September 1, 2007

Documentaries

The Secret - 2007

What the Bleep Do We Know!? - 2005

CPSIA information can be obtained
at www.ICGtesting.com
Printed in the USA
BVHW031418270819
556814BV00004B/728/P